Bruges – A Travel Guide of Art and History

A comprehensive guide to the architecture, churches and art galleries of Bruges, Belgium

Maxime Jensens

© Maxime Jansens 2016

All rights reserved. No text of this publication may be reproduced, distributed, or transmitted in any form or by any means, including photocopying, recording, or other electronic or mechanical methods, without the prior written permission of the publisher, except in the case of brief quotations embodied in critical reviews and certain other non-commercial uses permitted by copyright law.

This book features the work of several independent, private photographers and artists. Where appropriate, they have been attributed for their work. Images used under any Creative Commons and GNU free license remain under their respective licenses. No copyright or trademark infringement is intended by the imagery displayed within this book.

Cover image credit: Steppelandstock

Acknowledgments

I would chiefly like to thank my tutor and friend Pierre Durand for fostering my interest and knowledge in the representation of history in civic buildings. The many tour guides, tourism bureau clerks, and individuals I have encountered during my tours of the country I am proud to call my home also deserve due credit for their illuminating advice. Finally, I appreciate the help rendered by administrators of the attractions in Bruges, whose clarifications were invaluable in the completion of this guide.

About the Author

Growing up in Brussels, Maxime Jensens developed a keen interest and sense of the historic legacies which underpin the towns of his nation. As a child, he beheld the many stunning achievements in architecture and art, whether they be on the parts of institutions such as the Christian church or individually prolific artists, sculptors or architects. Noting how these beautiful attributes seldom fail to awe visitors with their uniqueness, Jensens ambitiously aimed to make a career from their depiction, accurately relaying of the past which so underpins his home nation.

Formerly a student of art history, Jensens today acts as a lecturer and blogger studying the old cities of both Belgium and France. Fluent in both French and English, his stated aim is to increase the awareness, appreciation and regard for his country's art. It is to this end that this guide was published, for the benefit of visitors eager to plunge into the cultural bulwarks Belgium has to offer.

Introduction

The object and plan of this series of city guides is somewhat different from that of any other guides presently available. They do not compete or clash with such existing works; they are intended to supplement than supplant them. My purpose is not to direct the stranger through the streets and squares of a Flemish town towards the buildings or sights which he may desire to visit; still less is it my intention to give him practical information about hotels, taxi fares, trains, tramways, and other every-day visiting conveniences. For such details, the traveller must still have recourse to the trusty pages of other, more general and utilitarian guides.

My desire rather is to supply the tourist who wishes to use his travel as a means of culture with such historical and antiquarian information as will enable him to understand, and therefore enjoy the architecture, sculpture, painting, and minor arts of the towns he visits. In one word, it is my object to give the reader in a very compendious form the result of all those inquiries which have naturally suggested themselves to my own mind during thirty-five years of foreign travel, the solution of which has cost myself a good deal of research, thought, and labour, beyond the facts which I could find in the everyday tour guide handbooks.

For several years past I have devoted myself to collecting and arranging material for a set of books to embody the idea I had thus entertained. I earnestly hope they may meet a want on the part of tourists, especially Americans, who, so far as my experience goes, usually come to Europe with an honest and reverent desire to learn from the Old World whatever of value it has to teach them, and who are prepared to take an amount of pains in turning their trip to good account which is both rare and praiseworthy. For such readers I shall call attention at times to other sources of information.

The market square and Belfry of Bruges - Image: Wolfgang Staudt

This guide book will deal more particularly with the city of Bruges, where heritage architecture, objects of art and other antiquities are numerous. In every one of them, the general plan pursued will be somewhat as follows. First will come the inquiry why a town ever gathered together at all at that particular spot—what induced the aggregation of human beings rather there than elsewhere. Next, we shall consider why that town grew to social or political importance and what the stages were by which it assumed its present shape. Thirdly, we shall ask why it gave rise to that higher form of handicraft which we know as Art, and towards what particular arts it especially gravitated. After that, we shall take in detail the various strata of its growth or development, examining the buildings and works of art which they contain in historical order, and, as far as possible, tracing the causes which led to their evolution. In particular, we shall lay stress upon the origin and meaning of each structure as an organic whole, and upon the allusions or symbols which its fabric embodies.

A single instance will show the method upon which I intend to proceed better than any amount of general description. A church, as a rule, is built over the body or relics of a particular saint, in whose special honour it was originally erected. That saint was usually one of great local importance at the moment of its erection, or was peculiarly implored against plague, foreign enemies, or some other pressing and dreaded misfortune. In dealing with such a church I endeavour to show what the circumstances were which led to its construction, and what memorials of these circumstances it still retains. In other cases it may derive its origin from some special monastic body—Benedictine, Dominican, Franciscan—and may therefore be full of the peculiar symbolism and historical allusion of the order who founded it. Wherever I have to deal with such a church, I try as far as possible to exhibit the effect which its origin had upon its architecture and decoration; to trace the image of the patron saint in sculpture or stained glass throughout the fabric; and to set forth the connection of the whole design with time and place, with order and purpose. In short, instead of looking upon monuments of the sort mainly as the product of this or that architect, I look upon them rather as material embodiments of the spirit of the age—crystallizations, as it were, in stone and bronze, in form and colour, of great popular enthusiasms.

By thus concentrating attention on what is essential and important in a town, I hope to give in a comparatively short space, though with inevitable conciseness, a fuller account than is usually given of the chief architectural and monumental works of the principal art-cities.

The famous Christmas Market of Bruges - Image: DimiTalen

As regards the character of the information given, it will be mainly historical, antiquarian, and, above all, explanatory. I am not a connoisseur—an adept in the difficult modern science of distinguishing the handicraft of various masters, in painting or sculpture, by minute signs and delicate inferential processes. In such matters, I shall be well content to follow the lead of the most authoritative experts. Nor am I an art-critic—a student versed in the technique of the studios and the dialect of the modeling-room. In such matters, again, I shall attempt little more than to accept the general opinion of the most discriminative judges. What I aim at rather is to expound the history and meaning of each work—to put the intelligent reader in such a position that he may judge for himself of the aesthetic beauty and success of the object before him. To recognise the fact that this is a Perseus and Andromeda, that a St. Barbara enthroned, the other an obscure episode in the legend of St. Philip, is not art-criticism, but it is often an almost indispensable prelude to the formation of a right and sound judgment. We must know what the artist was trying to represent before we can feel sure what measure of success he has attained in his representation.

I cannot venture to hope that handbooks containing such a mass of facts as these will be wholly free from errors and misstatements, above all in early editions. I can only beg those who may detect any such to point them out, without unnecessary harshness, to the author, care of the publisher, and if possible to assign reasons for any dissentient opinion.

Table of Contents

Acknowledgments 3
About the Author 4
Introduction 5
How to Use this Guidebook 11
Origins of the Belgian Towns 13
Bruges 22
   Origins of Bruges 23
   The Heart of Bruges 29
      Old St. John's Hospital 47
   Walks through Bruges 65
      First Walk 65
      Second Walk 68
      Third Walk 70
      Fourth Walk 71
   The Churches 73
      St. Salvator 73
      Church of Our Lady 82
      The Church of Saint Jacob / Sint-Jakobsberk 92
Historical Notes on Belgium 108

How to Use this Guidebook

As noted already, the guidance within this book does not profess to supply practical information in aid of transport, dining, accommodation, guided tours or general sightseeing, but rather is intended to enlighten the visitor about the old town and interesting items of culture, history and art said locale harbours. As such, it is best suited as a companion to a more general guidebook, enhancing and conferring depth in matters artistic and cultural.

You can happily read this book at leisure at home prior to your journey to Bruges. The sections upon specific art galleries or attractions however are best read while you explore and view each respective building and its contents. Individual artworks and artifacts are described, while descriptions upon their creators also feature.

Portions relating to each principal objects of art should be quietly read and digested before a visit, and referred to again afterwards. The portion to be read on the spot is made as brief as possible. For eBook readers it is advised to read with a large font size so as to be easily read in the dim light of churches, chapels, and galleries. Those with editions in print may benefit from reasonably sized, 12 point fonts. Where objects are numbered, the numbers used are always those of the latest official catalogues.

Individual works of merit are distinguished by an asterisk (*); those of very exceptional interest and merit have two asterisks. Undistinguished art of little notability is omitted, so that the tourist may appreciate works of renown.

As for touring advice, you should little at a time, and see it thoroughly. Never attempt to "do" any place or any monument in a quick, whirlwind tour characterized by brief milling around. By following strictly the order in which objects are noticed in this book, you will gain a conception of the historical evolution of the town which you cannot obtain if you go about looking at churches and palaces haphazardly.

This book does not profess to be an exhaustive account of the art and architecture present in Belgian cities. Its focus is mainly on the ancient heritage art and architecture of the medieval, renaissance and baroque periods, which together span epochs between the 12th and 18th century. These fruitful centuries birthed much of the best and most beautiful Belgian art and architecture, the styles of which remain with ease the most associated with the country and each of its significant cities.

Clearer memories, enjoyment and appreciation of the architecture and art of Belgium's principle art galleries and churches is what this book intends to convey, in contrast to ordinary guides which lack focus and depth upon the important historical and cultural characteristics of the cities they focus upon. Where they merely brush over art of supreme importance, as if ticking boxes off a list – this book aims to interest the artistic tourist with due description and intensity.

In aid of this aim parts relating directly to the old town, galleries, church and cathedral interiors, this book acts as a walking tour. Concise descriptions and instructions are made, enlightening you as to when to stop and observe specific items of significance.

Origins of the Belgian Towns

The somewhat heterogeneous country which we now call Belgium formed part of Gaul under the Roman Empire. But though rich and commercial even then, it seems to have been relatively little Romanised; and in the beginning of the 5th century it was overrun by the Salic Franks, on their way towards Laon, Soissons, and Paris. When civilization began to creep northward again in the 9th century through the districts barbarised by the Teutonic invasion, it was the Frankish Charlemagne (Karl the Great) who introduced Roman arts afresh into the Upper and Lower Rhinelands.

The Rhine from Basle to Cologne was naturally the region most influenced by this new Roman revival; but as Charlemagne had his chief seat at Aix-la-Chapelle (Aachen), near the modern Belgian frontier, the western Frankish provinces were also included in the sphere of his improvements. When the kingdom of the Franks began to divide more or less definitely into the Empire and France, the Flemish region formed nominally part of the Neustrian and, later, of the French dominions. From a very early date, however, it was practically almost independent, and it became so even in name during its later stages. But Brabant (with Brussels) remained a portion of the Empire.

The Rhine constituted the great central waterway of mediæval Europe; the Flemish towns were its ports and its manufacturing centres. They filled in the 13th and 14th centuries much the same place that Liverpool, Glasgow, Manchester, and Birmingham fill in the 20th. Many causes contributed to this result. Flanders, half independent under its own Counts, occupied a middle position, geographically and politically, between France and the Empire; it was comparatively free from the disastrous wars which desolated both these countries, and in particular (see under Ghent) it largely escaped the long smouldering quarrel between French and English which so long retarded the development of the former. Its commercial towns, again, were not exposed on the open sea to the attacks of pirates or hostile fleets, but were safely ensconced in inland flats, reached by rivers or canals, almost inaccessible to maritime enemies. Similar conditions elsewhere early ensured peace and prosperity for Venice.

An ancient canal running through rural Belgium - Image: Arctic-Cycler

The canal system of Holland and Belgium began to be developed as early as the 12th century (at first for drainage), and was one leading cause of the commercial importance of the Flemish cities in the 14th. In so flat a country, locks are all but unnecessary. The two towns which earliest rose to greatness in the Belgian area were thus Bruges and Ghent; they possessed in the highest degree the combined advantages of easy access to the sea and comparative inland security. Bruges, in particular, was one of the chief stations of the Hanseatic League, which formed an essentially commercial alliance for the mutual protection of the northern trading centres. By the 14th century Bruges had thus become in the north what Venice was in the south, the capital of commerce. Trading companies from all the surrounding countries had their "factories" in the town, and every European king or prince of importance kept a resident minister accredited to the merchant Republic.

Some comprehension of the mercantile condition of Europe in general during the Middle Ages is necessary in order to understand the early importance and wealth of the Flemish cities. Southern Europe, and in particular Italy, was then still the seat of all higher civilization, more especially of the trade in manufactured articles and objects of luxury. Florence, Venice, and Genoa ranked as the polished and learned cities of the world. Further east, again, Constantinople still remained in the hands of the Greek emperors, or, during the Crusades, of their Latin rivals. A brisk trade existed viâ the Mediterranean between Europe and India or the nearer East. This double stream of traffic ran along two main routes—one, by the Rhine, from Lombardy and Rome; the other, by sea, from Venice, Genoa, Florence, Constantinople, the Levant, and India.

On the other hand, France was still but a half civilized country, with few manufactures and little external trade; while England was an exporter of raw produce, chiefly wool. The Hanseatic merchants of Cologne held the trade of London; those of Wisby and Lübeck governed that of the Baltic; Bruges, as head of the Hansa, was in close connection with all of these, as well as with

Hull, York, Novgorod, and Bergen. The position of the Flemish towns in the 14th century was thus not wholly unlike that of New York, Philadelphia, and Boston at the present day; they stood as intermediaries between the older civilized countries, like Italy or the Greek empire, and the newer producers of raw material, like England, North Germany, and the Baltic towns.

The Hunt of Maximilian tapestry

The local manufactures of Flanders consisted chiefly of woolen goods and linens; the imports included Italian luxuries, Spanish figs and raisins, Egyptian dates, Oriental silks, English wool, cattle, and metals, Rhenish wines, and Baltic furs, skins, and walrus tusks.

In the early 16th century, when navigation had assumed new conditions, and trade was largely diverted to the Atlantic, Antwerp, the port of the Schelde, superseded the towns on the inland network. As Venice sank, Antwerp rose.

The art that grew up in the Flemish cities during their epoch of continuous commercial development bears on its very face the visible impress of its mercantile origin. France is essentially a monarchical country, and it is centralized in Paris; everything in old French art is therefore regal and lordly. The Italian towns were oligarchies of nobles; so the principal buildings of Florence and Venice are the castles or palaces of the princely families, while their pictures represent the type of art that belongs in its nature to a cultivated aristocracy.

But in Flanders, everything is in essence commercial. The architecture consists mainly, not of private palaces, but of guilds, town halls, exchanges, belfries: the pictures are the portraits of solid and successful merchants, or the devotional works which a merchant donor presented to the patron saint of his town or business. They are almost overloaded with details of fur, brocade, jewelry, lace, gold, silver, polished brass, glasswork, Oriental carpets, and richly carved furniture. In order to understand Flemish art, therefore, it is necessary to bear in mind at every step that it is the art of a purely commercial people.

Another point which differentiates Flemish painting from the painting of Italy during the same period is the complete absence of any opportunity for the display of frescoes. In the Italian churches, where the walls serve largely for support, and the full southern light makes the size of the windows of less importance, great surfaces were left bare in the nave and aisles, or in the lower part of the choir, crying aloud for decoration at the hands of the fresco-painter. But in the northern Gothic, which aimed above all things at height and the soaring effect, and which almost annihilated the wall, by making its churches consist of rows of vast windows with intervening piers or buttresses, the opportunity for mural decoration occurred but seldom.

The climate also destroyed frescoes. Hence the works of pictorial art in Flemish buildings are almost confined to altar-pieces and votive tablets. Again, the great school of painting in early Italy (from Giotto to Perugino) was a school of fresco-painters; but in Flanders no high type of art arose till the discovery of oil-painting. Pictures were usually imported from the Rhine towns. Hence, pictorial art in the Low Countries seems to spring almost full-fledged, instead of being traceable through gradual stages of evolution as in Italy. Most of the best early paintings are small and highly finished; it was only at a comparatively late date, when Antwerp became the leading town, that Italian influence began to produce the larger and coarser canvases of Rubens and his followers.

Very early Flemish art greatly resembles the art of the School of Cologne. Only with Hubert and Jan van Eyck (about 1360-1440)

does the distinctively Flemish taste begin to show itself—the taste for delicate and minute workmanship, linked with a peculiar realistic idealism, more dainty than German work, more literal than Italian. It is an art that bases itself upon truth of imitation and perfection of finish: its chief æsthetic beauty is its jewel-like colour and its wealth of decorative adjuncts. The subsequent development of Flemish painting—the painting that pleased a clique of opulent commercial patrons—we shall trace in detail in the various cities.

Whoever wishes to gain a deeper insight into Flemish painting should take in his portmanteau Sir Martin Conway's "Early Flemish Artists," a brilliant and masterly work of the first importance, to which this Guide is deeply indebted.

The political history of the country during this flourishing period of the Middle Ages has also stamped itself, though somewhat less deeply, on the character of the towns and of the art evolved in them. The Counts of Flanders, originally mere lords of Bruges and its district, held their dominions of the Kings of France. Their territory included, not only Arras (at first the capital, now included in France) with Bruges, Ghent, Courtrai, Tournay, and Ypres, but also the towns and districts of Valenciennes, Lille, and St. Omer, which are now French. From the time of Baldwin VIII. (1191), however, Arras became a part of France, and Ghent was erected into the capital of Flanders. In the beginning of the 13th century, two women sovereigns ruled in succession; under them, and during the absence of the elective Counts on crusades, the towns rose to be practically burgher republics. Bruges, Ypres, Ghent, and Lille were said to possess each 40,000 looms; and though this is certainly a mediæval exaggeration, yet the Flemish cities at this epoch were at any rate the chief manufacturing and trading centres of northern Europe, while London was still a mere local emporium.

A statue of Jacob van Artevelde - Image: Demeester

In the 14th century, the cities acquired still greater freedom. The citizens had always claimed the right to elect their Count; and the people of Ghent now made treaties without him on their own account with Edward III. of England. To this age belongs the heroic period of the Van Arteveldes at Ghent, when the burghers became the real rulers of Flanders, as will be more fully described hereafter. In 1384 however, Count Louis III died, leaving an only daughter, who was married to Philip the Bold of Burgundy; and the wealthy Flemish towns thus passed under the sway of the powerful princes of Dijon. Brabant fell later by inheritance to Philip the Good. It was under the Burgundian dynasty, who often held their court at Ghent, that the arts of the Netherlands attained their first great development. Philip the Good (1419-1467) employed Jan van Eyck as his court painter; and during his reign or just after it the chief works of Flemish art were produced in Bruges, Ghent, Brussels, and Tournai.

Charles the Bold, the last Duke of Burgundy, left one daughter, Mary, who was married to Maximilian, afterwards Emperor. From that date forward the history of the Flemish towns is practically merged in that of the dynasty of Charles V., and finally becomes the story of an unwilling and ever justly rebellious Spanish province. The subsequent vicissitudes of Belgium as an Austrian appanage, a part of Holland, and an independent kingdom, belong to the domain of European history. For the visitor, it is the period of the Burgundian supremacy that really counts in the cities of Belgium.

Yet the one great point for the tourist to bear in mind is really this—that the art of the Flemish towns is essentially the art of a group of burgher communities. It is frankly commercial, neither royal nor aristocratic. In its beginnings it develops a strictly municipal architecture, with a school of painters who aimed at portraiture and sacred panel pictures. After the Reformation had destroyed sacred art in Holland, painting in that part of the Netherlands confined itself to portraits and to somewhat vulgar popular scenes: while in Belgium it was Italianised, or rather Titianised and Veronesed, by Rubens and his followers. But in its best days it was national, local, and sacred or personal.

Take Conway's "Early Flemish Artists" with you in your portmanteau, and read over in the evening his account of the works you have seen during the day.

Bruges

Panorama of Bruges' canals at Spiegelrei and Langerei – Image: Mark D. Hammond

The capital of West Flanders, Bruges situation in the Belgian northwest place it in proximity to the capital, with public transport well-developed. The centre, or *Groenerei*, is renowned for its beautiful canals and architectural marvels which span the centuries defining Gothic and Medieval styles. Many of the buildings lining the canals remain as they have for several centuries, and were granted the status of UNESCO World Heritage Site in 2000.

Given its undeniable beauty and juxtaposition of ancient history with the majesty of fine architecture, Bruges has become one of Belgium's most visited cities. For lovers of artwork and culture its beautiful streets, religious and monastic structures offer a wondrous opportunity to soak up a defining history and centuries of artistic talent whose results manifest impressively.

The city has enjoyed popularity, featured in such films as *In Bruges*, and *The Monuments Men*. Its presence in literary works and in documentaries of the wider European continent further serves to elevate its profile, with resultant rises in visitor numbers providing prosperity to the town and its people.

Origins of Bruges

In a lost corner of the great lowland flat of Flanders, defended from the sea by an artificial dyke, and at the point of intersection of an intricate network of canals and waterways, there arose in the early Middle Ages a trading town, known in Flemish as Brugge, in French as Bruges (that is to say, The Bridge), from a primitive structure that here crossed the river. (A number of bridges now span the sluggish streams. All of them open in the middle to admit the passage of shipping.) Bruges stood originally on a little river, the Reye, once navigable, now swallowed by canals: and the Reye flowed into the Zwin, long silted up, but then the safest harbour in the Low Countries.

Bruge and its belfry - Image: Hans Hillewaert

At first the capital of a petty Count, this land-locked internal harbour grew in time to be the Venice of the North, and to gather round its quays, or at its haven of Damme, the ships and merchandise of all neighbouring peoples. Already in 1200 it ranked as the central mart of the Hanseatic League. It was the port of entry for English wool and Russian furs: the port of departure for Flemish broadcloths, laces, tapestries, and linens. Canals soon connected it with Ghent, Dunkirk, Sluys, Furnes, and Ypres. Its nucleus lay in a little knot of buildings about the Grand' Place and the Hôtel de Ville, stretching out to the Cathedral and the Dyver; thence it spread on all sides till in 1362 it filled the whole space within the existing ramparts, now largely abandoned or given over to fields and gardens. It was the wealthiest town of Europe, outside Italy. In the 14th century, Bruges was frequently the residence of the Counts of Flanders; and in the 15th it became the seat of the brilliant court of the Dukes of Burgundy. Under their rule, the opulent burghers and foreign merchants began to employ a group of famous artists who have made the city a place of pilgrimage for Europe and America, and to adorn the town with most of those buildings which now beautify its decay.

The foreign traders in Bruges lived in "factories" or guilds, resembling monasteries or colleges, and were governed by their own commercial laws. The Bardi of Florence were among its famous merchants: the Medici had agents here: so had the millionaire Fuggers of Augsburg.

Bruges is the best place in which to make a first acquaintance with the towns and art of Flanders, because here almost all the principal buildings are mediæval, and comparatively little that is modern comes in to mar the completeness of the picture. We see in it the architecture and the painting of Flanders, in the midst of the houses, the land, and the folk that gave them origin. Brussels is largely modernised, and even Ghent has great living manufactures; but Bruges is a fossil of the 15th century. It was the first to flourish and the first to decay of the towns of Belgium.

Bruges canals and parkland - Image: Rodrigo Menezes

The decline of the town was due partly to the break-up of the Hanseatic system; partly to the rise of English ports and manufacturing towns; but still more (and especially as compared with other Flemish cities) to the silting of the Zwin, and the want of adaptation in its waterways to the needs of great ships and modern navigation. The old sea entrance to Bruges was through the Zwin, by way of Sluys and Kadzand; up that channel came the Venetian merchant fleet and the Flemish galleys, to the port of Damme. By 1470, it ceased to be navigable for large vessels. The later canal is still open, but as it passes through what is now Dutch territory, it is little used; nor is it adapted to any save ships of comparatively small burden. Another canal, suitable for craft of 500 tons, leads through Belgian territory to Ostend; but few vessels now navigate it, and those for the most part only for local trade. The town has shrunk to half its former size, and has only a quarter of its mediæval population. The commercial decay of Bruges, however, has preserved its charm for the artist, the archeologist, and the tourist; its sleepy streets and unfrequented quays are among the most picturesque sights of bustling and industrial modern Belgium. The great private palaces, indeed, are almost all destroyed: but many public buildings remain, and the domestic architecture is quaint and pretty.

Jan Van Eyck - Ardolfini portrait

Bruges was the mother of the arts in Flanders. Jan van Eyck lived here from 1428 to 1440: Memling, probably, from 1477 till 1494. Caxton, the first English printer, lived as a merchant at Bruges (in the Domus Anglorum or English factory) from 1446 to

1476, and probably put in the press here the earliest English printed book (though strong grounds have been adduced in favour of Cologne). Colard Mansion, the great printer of Bruges at that date, was one of the leaders in the art of typography.

Those who desire further information on this most interesting town will find it in James Weale's Bruges et ses Environs, an admirable work, to which I desire to acknowledge my obligations.

Procession of the Holy Blood - Image: Alberto Fernandez Fernandez

At least two whole days should be devoted to Bruges: more if possible. But the hasty traveller, who has but time for a glimpse, should neglect the churches, and walk round the Grand' Place and the Place du Bourg to the Dyver: spending most of his time at the **Hôpital de St. Jean, which contains the glorious works of Memling. These are by far the most important objects to be seen in the city. The description in this Guide is written from the point of view of the more leisurely traveller.

Expect the frequent recurrence of the following symbols on houses or pictures: (1) the Lion of Flanders, heraldic or otherwise, crowned, and bearing a collar with a pendant cross; (2) the Bear of Bruges; (3) the Golden Fleece (Toison d'or), the device of the Order founded by Philippe le Bon in 1430, and appropriate to a country which owed its wealth to wool; it consists of a sheep's skin suspended from a collar. The Flemish emblem of the Swan is also common as a relief or decoration.

St. Donatian, Archbishop of Rheims, is the patron saint. His mark is a wheel with five lighted candles.

The Heart of Bruges

The original nucleus of Bruges is formed by the Place du Bourg, which stands near the centre of the modern city. In 865, Baldwin Bras-de-Fer, Count of Flanders, built a château or burg by the Reye, in a corner of land still marked by the modern canal of the Dyver, and near it a chapel, into which he transported the relics of St. Donatian.

Place du Bourg - Image: Donar Reiskoffer

This burg grew in time into the chief palace of the Counts of Flanders, now replaced by the Palais de Justice; while the chapel by its side developed into the first cathedral of Bruges, St. Donatian, now wholly demolished. A bridge hard by crossed the little river Reye; and from this bridge the town ultimately derives its name. The burg was built as a tête-du-pont to protect the passage. A town of traders gradually sprang up under the protection of the castle, and developed at last into the great trading port of Bruges. To this centre, then, we will first direct ourselves.

Go from your hotel, down the Rue St. Amand, or the Rue St. Jacques, to the Grand' Place or market-place of Bruges, noticing on your way the numerous handsome old houses, with high-pitched roofs and gable-ends arranged like steps, mostly of the 16th and 17th centuries. (Bruges is a Flemish-speaking town: note the true names of the streets in Flemish.)

The belfry in Bruges Markt - Image: L. Ellis

The very tall square tower which faces you as you enter the Grand' Place is the *Belfry, the centre and visible embodiment of the town of Bruges. The Grand' Place itself was the forum and meeting-place of the soldier-citizens, who were called to arms by the chimes in the Belfry. The centre of the Place is therefore appropriately occupied by a colossal statue group (modern) of Pieter de Coninck and Jan Breidel, the leaders of the citizens of Bruges at the Battle of the Spurs before the walls of Courtrai in 1302, a conflict which secured the freedom of Flanders from the interference of the Kings of France. The group is by Devigne. The reliefs on the pedestal represent scenes from the battle and its antecedents.

The majestic Belfry itself represents the first beginnings of freedom in Bruges. Leave to erect such a bell-tower, both as a mark of independence and to summon the citizens to arms, was one of the first privileges which every Teutonic trading town desired to wring from its feudal lord. This (brick) tower, the pledge of municipal rights, was begun in 1291 (to replace an earlier one of wood), and finished about a hundred years later, the octagon (in stone) at the summit (which holds the bells) having been erected in 1393-96. It consists of three stories, the two lower of which are square and flanked by balconies with turrets; the windows below are of the simple Early Gothic style, but show a later type of architecture in the octagon. The niche in the centre contains the Virgin and Child (restored, after being destroyed by the French revolutionists). Below it on either side are smaller figures holding escutcheons. From the balcony between these last, the laws and the rescripts of the Counts were read aloud to the people assembled in the square.

The Belfry can be ascended by steps. Apply to the concierge; 25 c. per person. Owing to the force of the wind, it leans slightly to the S.E. The *view from the top is very extensive and striking; it embraces the greater part of the Plain of Flanders, with its towns and villages: the country, though quite flat, looks beautiful when thus seen. In early times, however, the look-out from the summit was of practical use for purposes of observation, military or maritime. It commanded the river, the Zwin, and the sea approach by Sluys and Damme; the course of the various canals; and the roads to Ghent, Antwerp, Tournai, and Courtrai. The Belfry contains a famous set of chimes, the mechanism of which may be inspected by the visitor. He will have frequent opportunities of hearing the beautiful and mellow carillon, perhaps to excess. The existing bells date only from 1680: the mechanism from 1784.

The Halle en Belfort adjacent to the Belfry – Image: Smabs Sputzer

The square building on either side of the Belfry, known as Les Halles, was erected in or about 1248, and is a fine but sombre specimen of Early Gothic civic architecture. The wing to the left was originally the Cloth Hall, for the display and sale of the woollen manufactures of Ghent and Bruges. It is now used as municipal offices. A door to the left gives access to a small Museum of Antiquities on the ground floor, which may be safely neglected by all save specialist archæologists. The wing to the right is the meat market.

Now, stand with your back to the Belfry to survey the Square. The brick building on your right is the Post Office (modern); the stone one beyond it (also modern) is the Palace of the Provincial Government of Flanders. Both have been erected in a style suitable to the town. In the Middle Ages, ships could come up to this part of the Grand' Place to discharge their cargo. The quaint houses that face you, with high-pitched gable-ends, are partly modern, but mostly old, though restored. On the left (W.) side of the Place, at the corner of the Rue St. Amand, stands the square castle-like building known as Au Lion de Flandre and marked by its gold crest bearing lion.

Lion des Flanders statue - Image: Ludovic Péron

It is one of the best brick mediæval buildings in Bruges. According to a doubtful tradition, it was occupied by Charles II. of England during his exile, when he was created by the

Brugeois King of the Crossbowmen of St. Sebastian (see later). In the house beside it, known as the Craenenburg, the citizens of Bruges imprisoned Maximilian, King of the Romans, from the 5th to the 17th of February, 1488, because he would not grant the care of his son Philip, heir to the crown of the Netherlands, to the King of France. They only released him after he had sworn before an altar erected at the spot, on the Host, the true Cross, and the Relics of St. Donatian, to renounce his claim to the guardianship of his son, and to grant a general amnesty. However, he was treacherously released from his oath by a congress of Princes convened a little later by his father, the Emperor Frederic IV.

Bruges Provincial Government Palace and Post Office - Image: Brian Snelson

From the corner of the Post Office, take the short Rue Breydel to the Place du Bourg, the still more intimate centre and focus of the early life of Bruges. This Place contained the old Palace of the Counts of Flanders, and the original Cathedral, both now destroyed, as well as the Town Hall and other important buildings still preserved for us.

The tallest of the three handsome edifices on the S. side of the Square (profusely adorned with sculpture) is the **Hôtel de Ville, a beautiful gem of Middle Gothic architecture, begun about 1376, and finished about 1387. This is one of the finest pieces of civic architecture in Belgium. The façade, though over-restored, and the six beautiful turrets and chimneys, are in the main of the original design. The sculpture in the niches, destroyed during the French Revolution, has been only tolerably replaced by modern Belgian sculptors in our own day. The lower tier contains the Annunciation, on the right and left of the doorway, with figures of various saints and prophets. In the tiers above this are statues of the Counts of Flanders of various ages. The reliefs just below the windows of the first floor represent episodes from Biblical history:—David before Saul, David dancing before the Ark, the Judgment of Solomon, the Building of Solomon's Temple, and other scenes which the visitor can easily identify. The Great Hall in the interior is interesting only for its fine pendant Gothic wooden roof.

Bruges City Hall - Image: Wolfgang Staudt

The somewhat lower building, to the right of the Hôtel de Ville (Stadhuis, or City Hall), is the **Chapelle du Saint Sang. The decorated portal round the corner also forms part of the same building.

In the 12th and 13th centuries (age of the Crusades) the chivalrous and credulous knights of the North and West who repaired to the Holy Land, whether as pilgrims or as soldiers of the Faith, were anxious to bring back with them relics of the saints or of still more holy personages. The astute Greeks and Syrians with whom they had to deal rose to the occasion, and sold the simple Westerns various sacred objects of more or less doubtful authenticity at fabulous prices. Over these treasured deposits stately churches were often raised; for example, St. Louis of France constructed the Sainte Chapelle in Paris, to contain the Crown of Thorns and part of the True Cross, which he had purchased at an immense cost from Baldwin, Emperor of Constantinople.

Among the earlier visitors to the Holy Land who thus signalised their journey was Theodoric of Alsace, elected Count of Flanders in 1128; he brought back with him in 1149 some drops of the Holy Blood of the Saviour, said to have been preserved by Joseph of Arimathea, which he presented to his faithful city of Bruges. Fitly to enshrine them, Theodoric erected a chapel in the succeeding year, 1150; and this early church forms the lower floor of the existing building. Above it, in the 15th century, when Bruges grew richer, was raised a second and more gorgeous chapel (as at the Sainte Chapelle), in which the holy relic is now preserved. Almost all the works of art in the dainty little oratory accordingly bear special reference to the Holy Blood, its preservation, and its transport to Bruges. The dedication is to St. Basil, the founder of eastern monasticism—a Greek Father little known in the West, whose fame Theodoric must have learned in Syria. The nobles of Flanders, it must be remembered, were particularly active in organising the Crusades.

Basilica of the Holy Blood - Image: Jim Linwood

The exterior has a fine figure of St. Leonard (holding the fetters which are his symbol) under a Gothic niche. He was the patron of Christian slaves held in duress by the Saracens. The beautiful flamboyant portal and staircase, round the corner, erected in 1529-1533, in the ornate decorative style of the period, have (restored) figures of Crusaders and their Queens in niches, with incongruous Renaissance busts below.

The Museum of the Brotherhood of the Holy Blood, on the first floor, which we first visit, contains by the left wall the handsome silver-gilt Reliquary (of 1617), studded with jewels, which encloses the drops of the Holy Blood. The figures on it represent Christ (the source of the Blood), the Blessed Virgin, St. Basil (patron of the church), and St. Donatian (patron of the town). The Blood is exhibited in a simpler châsse in the chapel every Friday; that is to say, on the day of the Crucifixion. The great Reliquary itself is carried in procession only, on the Monday after the 3rd of May. Right and left of the châsse are portraits of the members of the Confraternity of the Holy Blood by P. Pourbus, 1556: unusually good works of this painter. A triptych to the right, by an unknown master of the early 16th century, figures the Crucifixion, with special reference to the Holy Blood, representing St. Longinus in the act of piercing the side of Christ (thus drawing the Blood), with the Holy Women and St. John in attendance; on the wings, the Way to Calvary, and the Resurrection.

The altar upon which the Holy Blood relic is presented - Image: Matt Hopkins

Between the windows is a curious chronological picture of the late 15th century, representing the History of Our Lady in the usual stages, with other episodes. To the right of it, a painting of the 15th century shows Count Theodoric receiving the Holy Blood from his brother-in-law, Baldwin, King of Jerusalem, and the bringing of the Holy Blood to Bruges.

On the right wall there is a famous *triptych by Gerard David (the finest work here), representing the Deposition in the Tomb, with the Maries, St. John, Nicodemus, and an attendant holding a dish to contain the Holy Blood, which is also seen conspicuously flowing from the wounds; the left wing shows the Magdalen with Cleophas; the right wing, the preservation of the Crown of Thorns by Joseph of Arimathea. The portrait character of the faces is admirable: stand long and study this fine work.

The original designs for the windows of the Chapel are preserved in a glass case by the window; behind which are fragments of early coloured glass; conspicuous among them, St. Barbara with her tower. On the exit wall is a fine piece of late Flemish tapestry, representing the bringing of the body of St. Augustine to Pavia, with side figures of San Frediano of Lucca and Sant' Ercolano of Perugia—executed, no doubt, for an Italian patron.

Basilica of the Holy Blood - main nave

The Chapel itself, which we next enter, is gorgeously decorated in polychrome, recently restored. The stained glass windows, containing portraits of the Burgundian Princes from the beginning of the dynasty down to Maria Theresa and Francis I., were executed in 1845 from earlier designs. The large window facing the High Altar is modern. It represents appropriately the history of the Passion, the origin of the Sacred Blood, its Transference to Bruges, and the figures of the Flemish Crusaders engaged in its transport. At the summit of the window, notice the frequent and fitting symbol of the pelican feeding its young with its own blood.

In the little side chapel to the right, separated from the main building by an arcade of three arches, is the tabernacle or canopy from which the Sacred Blood is exhibited weekly. To the right is hung a Crown of Thorns. Notice, also, the Crown of Thorns held by the angel at the top of the steps. The window to the left (modern) represents St. Longinus, the centurion who pierced the side of Christ, and St. Veronica, displaying her napkin which she gave to the Saviour to wipe his face on the way to Calvary, and which retained ever after the impress of the Divine Countenance. Almost all the other objects in the chapel bear reference, more or less direct, to the Holy Blood. Observe particularly in the main chapel the handsome modern High Altar with its coloured reliefs of scenes of the Passion. Such scenes as the Paschal Lamb on its base, with the Hebrew smearing the lintel of the door, are of course symbolical.

The Lower Chapel, to which we are next conducted, is a fine specimen of late Romanesque architecture. It was built by Theodoric in 1150. Its solid short pillars and round arches contrast with the lighter and later Gothic of the upper building. The space above the door of the eastern of the two chapels which face the entrance is occupied by an interesting mediæval relief representing a baptism with a dove descending. Notice as you pass out, from the Place outside, the two beautiful turrets at the west end of the main chapel.

Oude Civiele Griffie - Image: PMRMaeyaert

To the left of the Hôtel de Ville stands the ornate and much gilded Renaissance building known as the *Maison de l'Ancien Greffe – or Oude Civiele Griffie - originally the municipal record office. It bears the date 1537, and received due restoration complete with profuse gold decoration. Over the main doorway is the Lion of Flanders; on the architrave of the first floor are heads of Counts and Countesses; and the building is surmounted by a figure of Justice, with Moses and Aaron and emblematical statues. Note the Golden Fleece and other symbols. The interior is uninteresting.

Palais du justice - Image: sailko

The east side of the square is formed by the Palais de Justice, which stands on the site of an old palace of the Counts of Flanders, presented by Philippe le Beau to the Liberty of Bruges, and employed by them as their town hall of the Buitenpoorters, or inhabitants of the district outside the gate, known as the Franc de Bruges. The Renaissance building, erected between 1520 and 1608, was burnt down and replaced in the 18th century by the very uninteresting existing building. Parts of the old palace, however, were preserved, one room in which should be visited for the sake of its magnificent **chimney-piece. In order to see it, enter the quadrangle: the porter's room faces you as you enter.

The concierge conducts you to the Court-Room, belonging to the original building. Almost the entire side of the room is occupied by a splendid Renaissance chimney-piece, executed in 1529, after designs by Lancelot Blondeel of Bruges (a painter whose works are frequent in the town), and Guyot de Beaugrant of Malines, for the Council of the Liberty of Bruges, in honour of Charles V., as a memorial of the Treaty of Cambrai, in 1526. (This was the treaty concluded after the battle of Pavia, by which François Ier of France was compelled to acknowledge the independence of Flanders. Some of the figures in the background are allusive to the victory.) The lower part, or chimney-piece proper, is of black marble. The upper portion is of carved oak.

The marble part has four bas-reliefs in white alabaster by Guyot de Beaugrant, representing the History of Susannah, a mere excuse for the nude: (1) Susannah and the Elders at the Bath; (2) Susannah dragged by the Elders before the Judge; (3) Daniel before the Judge exculpating Susannah; (4) The Stoning of the Elders. The genii at the corners are also by Beaugrant. The whole is in the pagan taste of the Renaissance. The upper portion in oak contains in the centre a statue of Charles V., represented in his capacity as Count of Flanders (as shown by the arms on his cuirass): the other figures represent his descent and the accumulation of sovereignties in his person. On the throne behind Charles (ill seen) are busts of Philippe le Beau, his father, through whom he inherited the Burgundian dominions, and Johanna (the Mad) of Spain, his mother, through whom he inherited the united Peninsula.

The statues left and right are those of his actual royal predecessors. The figures to the left are his paternal grandfather, the Emperor Maximilian, from whom he derived his German territories, and his paternal grandmother, *Mary of Burgundy, who brought into the family Flanders, Burgundy, etc. Mary is represented with a hawk on her wrist, as she was killed at twenty-five by a fall from her horse while out hawking. (We shall see her tomb later at Notre-Dame.) The figures on the right are those of Ferdinand of Aragon and Isabella of Castile, the maternal grandfather and grandmother of Charles, from whom he inherited the two portions of his Spanish dominions. The medallions at the back represent the personages most concerned in the Treaty of Cambrai, and the Victory of Pavia which rendered it possible. (De Lannoy, the conqueror, to whom François gave up his sword, and Margaret of Austria.) The tapestry which surrounds the hall is modern; it was manufactured at Ingelmünster after the pattern of a few old fragments found in the cellars of the ancient building. The mediocre painting on the wall depicts a sitting of the court of the Liberty of Bruges in this room (1659).

The north side of the square is now occupied by a small Place planted with trees. Originally, however, the old cathedral of Bruges occupied this site. It was dedicated to St. Donatian, the patron of the city, whose relics were preserved in it; but it was barbarously destroyed by the French Revolutionary army in 1799, and the works of art which it contained were dispersed or ruined. Figures of St. Donatian occur accordingly in many paintings at Bruges. Jan van Eyck was buried in this cathedral, and a statue has been erected to him under the trees in the little Place. In order, therefore, mentally to complete the picture of the Place du Bourg in the 16th century, we must imagine not only the Hôtel de Ville, the Chapelle du Saint Sang, and the Ancien Greffe in something approaching their existing condition, but also the stately cathedral and the original

Renaissance building of the Franc de Bruges filling in the remainder.

The Bridge on Blind Donkey Street - Image: Jim Linwood

An archway spans the space between the Ancien Greffe and the Hôtel de Ville. Take the narrow street which dives beneath it, looking back as you pass at the archway with its inscription of S.P.Q.B. (for Senatus Populusque Brugensis). The street then leads across a bridge over the river Reye or principal canal, and affords a good view of the back of the earlier portion of the Palais de Justice, with its picturesque brick turrets, and a few early arches belonging to the primitive palace. I recommend the visitor to turn to the right after crossing the bridge, traverse the little square, and make his way home by the bank of the Dyver and the church of Notre-Dame. The view towards the Hôtel de Ville and the Belfry, from the part of the Dyver a little to the east behind the Belfry, is one of the most picturesque and striking in Bruges.

Ferraris' map of Bruges, circa 1775, depicts the city's nucleus

Old St. John's Hospital

The Hospital of St. John, one of the most ancient institutions in Bruges, or of its kind in Europe, was founded not later than 1188, and still retains, within and without, its mediæval arrangement. Its Augustinian brothers and nuns tend the sick in the primitive building, now largely added to.

The exterior of the old hospital of Saint John – Image: Jean-Pol Grandmont

Exterior aside, it derives its chief interest for the tourist from its small Picture Gallery, the one object in Bruges which must above everything else be visited. This is the only place for studying in full the exquisite art of Memling, whose charming and poetical work is here more fully represented than elsewhere. In this respect the Hospital of St. John may be fitly compared with the two other famous "one-man shows" of Europe—the Fra Angelicos at San Marco in Florence, and the Giottos in the Madonna dell' Arena at Padua. Many of the pictures were painted for the institution which they still adorn; so that we have here the opportunity of seeing works of mediæval art in the precise surroundings which first produced them.

The three Hans Memling panels upon the St. John altar

Hans Memling, whose name is also written Memlinc and Memlin, etc. (long erroneously cited as Hemling; through a mistaken reading of the initial in his signature) is a painter of whom little is known, save his work; but the work is the man, and therefore amply sufficient. He was born about 1430, perhaps in Germany, and is believed to have been a pupil of Roger van der Weyden, the Brussels painter, whose work we shall see later at Antwerp and elsewhere. Mr. Weale has shown that he was a person of some wealth, settled at Bruges in his own house (about 1478), and in a position to lend money to the town. He died in 1495. His period of activity as a painter is thus coincident with the earlier work of Carpaccio and Perugino in Italy; and he died while Raphael was still a boy.

In relation to the artists of his own country, whose works we have still to see, Memling was junior by more than a generation to Jan van Eyck, having been born about ten years before Van

Eyck died; he was also younger by thirty years than Roger van der Weyden; and by twenty or thirty years than Dierick Bouts; but older by at least twenty than Gerard David. Memling has been called the Fra Angelico of Flanders; but this is only true so far as regards Fra Angelico's panel works; the saintly Frate, when he worked in fresco, adopted a style wholly different from that which he displays in his miniature-like altar-pieces. It would be truer to say that Memling is the Benozzo Gozzoli of the North: he has the same love of decorative adjuncts, and the same naïve delight in the beauty of external nature.

Before visiting the Hospital, it is also well to be acquainted in outline with the history of St. Ursula, whose châsse or shrine forms one of its greatest treasures. The Hospital possessed an important relic of the saint—her holy arm—and about 1480-1489 commissioned Memling to paint scenes from her life on the shrine destined to contain this precious deposit. The chest or reliquary which he adorned for the purpose forms the very best work of Memling's lifetime.

St. Ursula was a British (or Bretonne) princess, brought up as a Christian by her pious parents. She was sought in marriage by a pagan prince, Conon, said to be the son of a king of England. The English king, called Agrippinus in the legend, sent ambassadors to the king of Britain (or Brittany) asking for the hand of Ursula for his heir. But Ursula made three conditions: first, that she should be given as companions ten noble virgins, and that she herself and each of the virgins should be accompanied by a thousand maiden attendants; second, that they should all together visit the shrines of the saints; and third, that the prince Conon and all his court should receive baptism. These conditions were complied with; the king of England collected 11,000 virgins; and Ursula, with her companions, sailed for Cologne, where she arrived miraculously without the assistance of sailors (but Memling adds them). Here, she had a vision of an angel bidding her to repair to Rome, the threshold of the apostles.

From Cologne, the pilgrims went up the Rhine by boat, till they arrived at Basle, where they disembarked and continued their journey on foot over the Alps to Italy. At length they reached the Tiber, which they descended till they approached the walls of Rome. There, the Pope, St. Cyriacus, went forth with all his clergy in procession to meet them. He gave them his blessing, and lest the maidens should come to harm in so wicked a city, he had tents pitched for them outside the walls on the side towards Tivoli. Meanwhile, prince Conon had come on pilgrimage by a different route, and arrived at Rome on the same day as his betrothed. He knelt with Ursula at the feet of the Pope, and, being baptized, received in exchange the name of Ethereus.

After a certain time spent in Rome, the holy maidens bethought them to return home again. Thereupon, Pope Cyriacus decided to accompany them, together with his cardinals, archbishops, bishops, patriarchs, and many others of his prelates. They crossed the Alps, embarked again at Basle, and made their way northward as far as Cologne. Now it happened that the army of the Huns was at that time besieging the Roman colony; and the pagans fell upon the 11,000 virgins, with the Pope and their other saintly companions. Prince Ethereus was one of the first to die; then Cyriacus, the bishops, and the cardinals perished. Last of all, the pagans turned upon the virgins, all of whom they slew, save only St. Ursula. Her they carried before their king, who, beholding her beauty, would fain have wedded her. But Ursula sternly refused the offer of this son of Satan; whereupon the king, seizing his bow, transfixed her breast with three arrows. Hence her symbol is an arrow; also, she is the patroness of young girls and of virgins, so that her shrine is particularly appropriate in a nunnery.

Both sides of the shrine of Saint Ursula

Most of the bones of St. Ursula and her 11,000 virgins are preserved at Cologne, the city of her martyrdom, where they are ranged in cases round the walls of a church dedicated in her honour; but her arm is here, and a few other relics are distributed elsewhere.

From the Grand' Place, turn down the Rue des Pierres, the principal shopping street of Bruges, with several fine old façades, many of them dated. At the Place Simon Stévin turn to the left, and go straight on as far as the church of Notre-Dame. The long brick building with Gothic arches, on your right, is the **Hospital of St. John the Evangelist.

First, examine the brick Gothic exterior. Over the outer doorway is the figure of a bishop with a flaming heart, the emblem of St.

Augustine, this being an Augustinian hospital. Continue on to the original main portal (now bricked up) with a broken pillar, and two 13th century reliefs in the tympanum. That to the right represents the Death of the Virgin, with the Apostles grouped around, and the figure of the Christ receiving her naked new-born soul as usual. Above is the Coronation of Our Lady. That to the left seems like a reversed and altered replica of the same subject, with perhaps the Last Judgment above it. It is, however, so much dilapidated that identification is difficult. (Perhaps the top is a Glory of St. Ursula.) Go on as far as the little bridge over the canal, to inspect the picturesque river front of the Hospital.

The pictures are collected in the former Chapter-house of the Hospital, above the door of which is another figure of St. Augustine.

St. Johns Hospital entrance - Image: Navy8300

The centre of the room is occupied by the famous châsse or **shrine containing the arm of St. Ursula, a dainty little Gothic chapel in miniature. It is painted with exquisite scenes from the legend, by Memling, with all the charm of a fairy tale. He treats it as a poetical romance. Begin the story on the side towards the window. (For a penetrating criticism of these works, see Conway.)

1st panel, on the left: St. Ursula and her maidens, in the rich dress of the Burgundian court of the 15th century, arrive at Cologne, the buildings of which are seen in the background, correctly represented, but not in their true relations. In a window in the background to the right, the angel appears to St. Ursula in a vision.

2nd panel: the Virgins arrive at Basle and disembark from the ships. In the background, they are seen preparing to make their way, one by one, across the Alps, which rise from low hills at the base to snowy mountains. From another ship Conon and his knights are disembarking.

**3rd panel: (the most beautiful:) the Maidens arrive at Rome. In the distance they are seen entering the city through a triumphal arch; in the foreground, St. Ursula kneels before St. Cyriacus and his bishops, with their attendant deacons, all the faces having the character of portraits. (Note especially the fat and jolly ecclesiastic just under the arch.) At the same time, her betrothed, Conon, with his knights, arrives at Rome by a different road, and is seen kneeling in a red robe trimmed with rich fur beside St. Ursula. (Fine portrait faces of Conon and an old courtier behind him.) The Pope and his priests are gathered under the portals of a beautiful round-arched building, whose exquisite architecture should be closely examined. To the extreme right, the new converts and Conon receive baptism naked in fonts after the early fashion. In the background of this scene, St. Ursula receives the Sacrament. (She may be recognised throughout by her peculiar blue-and-white dress, with its open sleeves.) To the left of her, Conon makes confession. In this, as in the other scenes, several successive moments of the same episode are contemporaneously represented. Look long at it.

Now, turn round the shrine, which swings freely on a pivot, to see the scenes of the return journey.

1st panel: (beginning again at the left:) the Pope and his bishops and cardinals embark with St. Ursula in the boat at Basle on their way to Cologne. Three episodes are here conjoined: the Pope cautiously stepping into a ship; the Pope seated; the ship sailing down the Rhine. All the faces here, and especially the timid old Pope stepping into the boat, deserve careful examination. In the background, the return over the Alps.

*2nd panel: the Maidens and the Pope arrive at Cologne, where they are instantly set upon by the armed Huns. Conon is slain by the thrust of a sword, and falls back dying in the arms of St. Ursula. Many of the maidens are also slaughtered.

*3rd panel: continuous with the last, but representing a subsequent moment: the Martyrdom of St. Ursula. The King of the Huns, in full armour, at the door of his tent, bends his bow to shoot the blessed martyr, who has refused his advances. Around are grouped his knights in admirably painted armour. (Note the reflections.) All the scenes have the character of a mediæval romance. For their open-air tone and make-believe martyrdom, see Conway.

At the ends of the shrine are two other pictures, (1) *St. Ursula with her arrow, as the protectress of young girls, sheltering a number of them under her cloak (not, as is commonly said, the 11,000 Virgins). Similar protecting figures of the saint are common elsewhere (Cluny, Bologna, etc.). At the opposite end, (2) the Madonna and Child with an apple, and at her feet two Augustinian nuns of this Hospital, kneeling, to represent the devotion of the order.

The roof of the shrine is also decorated with pictures. (1) St. Ursula receiving the crown of martyrdom from God the Father, with the Son and the Holy Ghost; at the sides, two angels playing the mandoline and the regal or portable organ; (2) St. Ursula in Paradise, bearing her arrow, and surrounded by her maidens, who shared her martyrdom, together with the Pope and other ecclesiastics in the background. (This picture is largely borrowed from the famous one by Stephan Lochner on the High Altar of Cologne Cathedral, known as the Dombild. If you are going on to Cologne, buy a photograph of this now, to compare with Meister Stephan later. His altar-piece is engraved in Conway. If you have it with you, compare them.) At the sides are two angels playing the zither and the violin. (The angels are possibly by a pupil.)

I have given a brief description only of these pictures, but every one of them ought to be carefully examined, and the character of the figures and of the landscape or architectural background noted. You will see nothing lovelier in all Flanders.

Near the window by the entrance is a **Triptych, also by Memling, commissioned by Brother Jan Floreins of this Hospital. The central panel represents the Adoration of the Magi, which takes place, as usual, under a ruined temple fitted up as a manger. The Eldest of the Three Kings (according to precedent) is kneeling and has presented his gift; Joseph, recognisable (in all three panels) by his red-and-black robe, stands erect behind him, with the presented gift in his hands. The Middle-aged King, arrayed in cloth of gold, with a white tippet, kneels with his gift to the left of the picture. The Young King, a black man, as always, is entering with his gift to the right.

The three thus typify the Three Ages of Man, and also the three known continents, Europe, Asia, Africa. On the left hand side of this central panel are figured the donor, Jan Floreins, and his brother Jacob. (Members of the same family are grouped in the well-known "Duchâtel Madonna," also by Memling, in the Louvre.) To the right is a figure looking in at a window and wearing the yellow cap still used by convalescents of the

Hospital, (arbitrarily said to be a portrait of Memling.) The left panel represents the Nativity, with our Lady, St. Joseph, and two adoring angels. The right panel shows the Presentation in the Temple, with Simeon and Anna, and St. Joseph (in red and black) in the background. (The whole thus typifies the Epiphany of Christ; left, to the Blessed Virgin; centre, to the Gentiles; right, to the Jews.) The outer panels, in pursuance of the same idea, have figures, right, of St. John Baptist with the lamb (he pointed out Christ to the Jews), with the Baptism of Christ in the background; and left, St. Veronica, who preserved for us the features of our Lord, displaying his divine face on her napkin. The architectural frame shows the First Sin and the Expulsion from Paradise. Note everywhere the strong character in the men's faces, and the exquisite landscape or architectural backgrounds. Dated 1479. This is Memling's finest altar-piece: its glow of colour is glorious.

By the centre window, a *triptych, doubtfully attributed to Memling, represents, in the centre, the Deposition from the Cross, with the Holy Blood conspicuous, as might be expected in a Bruges work. In the foreground are St. John, the Madonna, and St. Mary Magdalene; in the background, the preparations for the Deposition in the Tomb. On the wings: left, Brother Adrian Reins, the donor, with his patron saint, Adrian, bearing his symbol, the anvil, on which his limbs were struck off, and with his lion at his feet; right, St. Barbara with her tower, perhaps as patroness of armourers. On the exterior wings, left, St. Wilgefortis with her tau-shaped cross; right, St. Mary of Egypt, with the three loaves which sustained her in the desert.

On the same stand is the beautiful *diptych by Memling, representing Martin van Nieuwenhoven adoring the Madonna. The left panel represents Our Lady and the Child, with an apple, poised on a beautifully painted cushion. A convex mirror in the background reflects the backs of the figures (as in the Van Eyck of the National Gallery). Through the open window is seen a charming distant prospect. The right panel has the fine portrait of the donor, in a velvet dress painted with extreme realism. Note the admirable prayer-book and joined hands. At his back, a stained glass window shows his patron, St. Martin, dividing his cloak for the beggar. Below, a lovely glimpse of landscape. This is probably Memling's most successful portrait. Dated 1487: brought here from the Hospice of St. Julian, of which Martin was Master.

In all Flemish art, observe now the wooden face of the Madonna—ultimately derived, I believe, from imitation of painted wooden figures, and then hardened into a type. As a rule, the Madonna is the least interesting part of all Flemish painting; and after her, the women, especially the young ones. The men's faces are best, and better when old: character, not beauty, is what the painter cares for. This is most noticeable in Van Eyck, but is true in part even of Memling.

At the end of the room is the magnificent *triptych painted by Memling for the High Altar of the Church of this Hospital. This is the largest of his works, and it is dedicated to the honour of the two saints (John the Evangelist and John the Baptist) who are patrons of the Hospital. The central panel represents Our Lady, seated in an exquisite cloister, on a throne backed with cloth of gold. To the right and left are two exquisite angels, one of whom plays a regal, while the other, in a delicious pale blue robe, holds a book for Our Lady. Two smaller angels, poised in air, support her crown. To the left, St. Catherine of Alexandria kneels as princess, with the broken wheel and the sword of her martyrdom at her feet. The Child Christ places a ring on her finger; whence the whole composition is often absurdly called "The Marriage of St. Catherine." It should be styled "The Altarpiece of the St. Johns." To the right is St. Barbara, calmly reading, with her tower behind her. When these two saints are thus combined, they represent the meditative and the active life (as St. Barbara was the patroness of arms:) or, more definitely, the clergy and the knighthood.

Hence their appropriateness to an institution, half monastic, half secular. In the background stand the two patron saints; St. John Baptist with the lamb (Memling's personal patron), to the left, and St. John the Evangelist with the cup and serpent, to the right. (For these symbols, see Mrs. Jameson.) Behind the Baptist are scenes from his life and preaching. He is led to prison, and his body is burned by order of Julian the Apostate. Behind the Evangelist, he is seen in the cauldron of boiling oil. The small figure in black to the right is the chief donor, Brother Jan Floreins, who is seen further back in his secular capacity as public gauger of wine, near a great crane, which affords a fine picture of mercantile life in old Bruges. The left wing represents the life of St. John the Baptist.

In the distance is seen the Baptism of Christ. In a room to the left, the daughter of Herodias dances before Herod. The foreground is occupied by the episode of the Decollation, treated in a courtly manner, very redolent of the Burgundian splendour. Figures and attitudes are charming: only, the martyrdom sinks into insignificance beside the princess's collar.

Other minor episodes may be discovered by inspection. (The episodes on either wing overflow into the main pictures.) The right wing shows St. John the Evangelist in Patmos, writing the Apocalypse, various scenes from which are realistically and too solidly represented above him, without poetical insight. Memling here attempts to transcend his powers. He has no sublimity. On the exterior of the wings are seen the four other members of the society who were donors of the altar-piece; Anthony Zeghers, master of the Hospital, with his patron, St. Anthony, known by his pig and tau-shaped crutch and bell: Jacob de Cueninc, treasurer, accompanied by his patron, St. James the Greater, with his pilgrim's staff and scallop-shell: Agnes Casembrood, mistress of the Hospital, with her patron, St. Agnes, known by her lamb: and Claire van Hulsen, a sister, with her patron, St. Clara. Dated, 1479.

By the entrance door is a Portrait of Marie Moreel, represented as a Sibyl. She was a daughter of Willem Moreel or Morelli, a patron of Memling, whom we shall meet again at the Museum.

This is a fine portrait of a solid, plain body, a good deal spoiled by attempted cleaning. It comes from the Hospice of St. Julian.

As you go out, cast a glance at the fine old brick buildings, and note the cleanliness of all the arrangements.

It would be wise to return for another look prior to departure, and you should not be satisfied with a single visit.

The other pictures and objects formerly exhibited in this Hospital have been transferred to the Potterie and another building. They need only be visited by those whose time is ample.

Two nuns walk toward the Béguinage - Image: Josep Renalias

After leaving the Hospital, I do not advise an immediate visit to the Academy. Let the Memlings first sink into your mind. But the walk may be prolonged by crossing the canal, and taking the second turning to the right, which leads (over a pretty bridge of three arches) to the Béguinage, a lay-nunnery for ladies who take no vows, but who live in monastic fashion under the charge of a Superior. Above the gateway is a figure of St. Elizabeth of Hungary, (to whom the church within is dedicated) giving alms to a beggar. She wears her crown, and carries in her hand the crown and book which are her symbol. Remember these,—they will recur later.

Pass under the gateway and into the grass-grown precincts for an external glimpse of the quiet old-world close, with its calm white-washed houses. The church, dedicated to St. Elizabeth, is uninteresting. This walk may be further prolonged by the pretty bank of the Lac d'amour or Minnewater as far as the external canal, returning by the ramparts and the picturesque Porte de Gand.

Walks through Bruges

The town of Bruges itself is more interesting, after all, than almost any one thing in it. Vary your day by giving up the morning to definite sightseeing, and devoting the afternoon to strolls through the town and neighbourhoods, in search of picturesqueness and photo opportunities. I include here a few stray hints for such casual rambles.

First Walk

Set out from the Grand' Place, and turn down the Rue Breydel to the Place du Bourg. Cross the Place by the statue of Jan van Eyck; traverse the Rue Philippe Stock; turn up the Rue des Armuriers a little to the right, and continue on to the Place St. Jean, with a few interesting houses.

The famed statue of Jan Van Eyck in Bruges - Image: Steven Lek

Note here and elsewhere, at every turn, the little statues of the Virgin and Child in niches, and the old signs on the fronts or gables. The interesting Gothic turret which faces you as you go belongs to the old 14th Century building called De Poorters Loodge, or the Assembly Hall of the Noble Citizens within the Gate, as opposed to those of the Franc de Bruges.

Continue on in the same direction to the Place Jan van Eyck, where you open up one of the most charming views in Bruges over the canal and quays. The Place is "adorned" by a modern statue of Jan van Eyck. The dilapidated building to your left is that of the Académie des Beaux-Arts which occupies the site of the Citizens' Assembly Hall: the ancient edifice was wholly rebuilt and spoilt in 1755, with the exception of the picturesque tower, best viewed from the base of the statue. Opposite you, as you emerge into the Place, is the charming Tonlieu or Custom House, whose decorated façade and portal (restored) bear the date 1477, with the arms of Pieter van Luxemburg, and the collar of the Golden Fleece. The dainty little neighbouring house to the left, now practically united with it, has a coquettish façade: the saints in the niches are St. George, St. John Baptist, St. Thomas à Becket, (or Augustine?) and St. John the Evangelist.

The Tonlieu – or old Tollhouse – was formerly fitted up as the Municipal Library. It contains illuminated manuscripts and examples of editions printed by Colard Mansion. All round the Place are other picturesque mediæval or Renaissance houses.

The little street to the right (diagonally) of the Tonlieu leads on to the Marché du Mercedi, now called Place de Memling, embellished by a statue of the great painter. Cross the Place diagonally to the Quai des Espagnoles (Madonna and Child in front of you) and continue along the quay, to the left, to the first bridge; there cross and go along the picturesque Quai des Augustins to the Rue Flamande. (Quaint little window to the left, as you cross the bridge.) Follow the Rue Flamande as far as the Theatre, just before reaching which you pass, right, a handsome mediæval stone mansion, (formerly the Guild of the Genoese Merchants,) with a relief over the door, representing St. George killing the Dragon, and the Princess Cleodolind looking on. At the Theatre, turn to the right, following the tram-line, and making your way back to the Grand' Place by the Rue des Tonneliers.

The Tonlieu - Tollhouse - of Bruges - Image: Dennis Jarvis

As early as 1362, Bruges acquired its existing size, and was surrounded by ramparts, which still in part remain. A continuous canal runs round these ramparts, and beyond it again lies an outer moat. Most of the old gates have unhappily been destroyed, but four still exist. These may be made the objects of interesting rambles.

Second Walk

Go from your hotel, or from the Grand Place, by the Rue Flamande, as far as the Rue de l'Académie. Turn along this to the right, into the Place Jan van Eyck, noting as you pass the Bear of Bruges at the corner of the building of the old Academy. Follow the quay straight on till you reach a second canal, near the corner of which, by the Rue des Carmes, is an interesting shop selling decorative items.

Take the long squalid Rue des Carmes to the right, past the ugly convent of the English Ladies, with its domed church in the most painful taste of the later Renaissance (1736). The mediæval brick building on your right, at the end of the street, is the late Gothic Guild-house of the Archers of St. Sebastian.

The Little Bear of Bruges - Image: Derek Winterborn

Its slender octagonal tower has a certain picturesqueness. (St. Sebastian was of course the patron of archery.) Charles II. of England (see under the Grand' Place) was a member of this society during his exile: his bust is preserved here. So also was the Emperor Maximilian. Continue to the ramparts, and mount the first hill, crowned by a windmill,—a scene of a type familiar to us in many later Dutch and Flemish pictures. A picturesque view of Bruges is obtained from this point: the octagonal Belfry, the square tower of St. Sauveur, (the Cathedral), the tapering brick spire of Notre-Dame, with its projecting gallery and the steeple of the new church of the Madeleine are all conspicuous in views from this side. Follow the ramparts to the right, to the picturesque Porte de Ste. Croix, and on past the barracks and the little garden to the Quai des Dominicains, returning by the Park and the Place du Bourg or the Dyver.

Third Walk

Set out by the Grand Place and the Place du Bourg; then follow the Rue Haute, with its interesting old houses, as far as the canal. Do not cross it, but skirt the quay on the further side, with the towers of St. Walburge and St. Gilles in front of you. At the bridge, diverge to the right, round the church of St. Anne, and the quaint little Church of Jerusalem, which contains an unimportant imitation of the Holy Sepulchre at Jerusalem, founded by a burgomaster of Bruges in the 15th century.

It is just worth looking at. Return to the bridge, and follow the quay straight on to the modern Episcopal Seminary and the picturesque old Hospice de la Potterie, which now harbours the Museum of Antiquities belonging to the Hospital of St. John. I do not advise a visit. (It contains third-rate early Flemish pictures, inferior tapestry, and a few pieces of carved oak furniture. The entrance is by the door just beyond the church, Number F, 79. The church itself is worth a minute's visit.) This walk passes many interesting old houses, which it is not necessary now to specify. Return by the Porte de Damme, and the opposite side of the same canal, to the Pont des Carmes, whence follow the pretty canal on the right to the Rue Flamande.

Fourth Walk

Take the Rue St. Jacques, and go straight out to the Porte d' Ostende, which forms an interesting picture. Cross the canal and outer moat, and traverse the long avenue, past the gasometers, as far as the navigable canal from Bruges to Ostend. Then retrace your steps to the gateway, and return by the ramparts and the Railway Station to the Rue Nord du Sablon.

These four walks combined will show you almost all that is externally interesting in the streets and canals of the city.

The original Palace of the Counts of Flanders, we saw, occupied the site of the Palais de Justice. Their later residence, the Cour des Princes, in a street behind the Hôtel du Commerce, has now entirely disappeared. Its site is filled by a large ornate modern building, belonging to the Sisters of the Sacred Heart, who use it as a school for girls.

The water-system of Bruges is also interesting. The original river Reye enters the town at the Minnewater, flows past the Hospital and the Dyver, and turns northward at the Bourg, running under arches till it emerges on the Place Jan van Eyck.

This accounts for the apparently meaningless way this branch seems to stop short close to the statue of Van Eyck: also, for the medieval ships unloading at the Grand' Place. The water is now mostly diverted along the canals and the moat by the ramparts, with the craft upon these waterways mainly orientated to leisure and tourism.

The Churches

As previously mentioned, the original Cathedral of Bruges - St. Donatian - was destroyed by the French in 1799. Despite this, the town still possesses two fine medieval churches of considerable pretensions, as well as several others of lesser importance. Though of very ancient foundation, the two principal churches in their existing form date only from the most flourishing period of Bruges, the 13th, 14th, and 15th centuries.

St. Salvator

[This church is open 7 days a week. From Monday to Saturday it admits guests from 10am to 1pm, and is closed between 1pm and 2pm for lunch. It is reopened each day from 2pm to 5:30pm. The exception is Saturday, when the church closes at 3:30pm.

On Sunday opening times are narrower; 11:30am to 12pm (a mere half hour) during mornings, and from 2pm to 5pm in the afternoon.

Admission is free; however the church administration is appreciative of donations which aid in maintaining the order of the church and its artworks.]

A principle place of worship in Bruges, St. Salvator is most known for its well-maintained organ and striking, numerous stained glass Gothic archways.

St. Salvator Cathedral - Image: Christoph Radtke

St. Salvator or St. Sauveur, the larger, was erected into the Cathedral after the destruction of St. Donatian, whose relics were transferred to it. To this, therefore, we will first direct ourselves.

Go down the Rue des Pierres as far as the cathedral, which replaces a very ancient church built by St. Eligius (St. Éloy) in 646.

Externally, the edifice, which is built of brick, has rather a heavy and cumbrous effect, its chief good features being the handsome square tower and the large decorated windows of the N. and S. Transepts. The Choir and its chapels have the characteristic French form of a chevêt. The main portal of the N. Transept has been robbed of its sculpture. The Choir is of the late 13th century: the Nave and Transept are mainly in the decorated style of the 14th.

The best entrance is near the tower on the north side. Walk straight on into the body of the Nave, by the archway in the heavy tower, so as to view the internal architecture as a whole. The Nave and single Aisles are handsome and imposing, though the windows on the S. side have been despoiled of their tracery. Notice the curious high-pointed Triforium (1362), between the arches of the Nave and the windows of the Clerestory. The Choir is closed by a strikingly ugly debased Renaissance or rococo Rood-Screen, (1682), in black-and-white marble, supporting the organ. It has a statue of God the Father by the younger Quellin. The whole of the interior has been decorated afresh in somewhat gaudy polychrome by Jean Béthune. The effect is on the whole not unpleasing.

St Salvator - Stained glass archway and panes. Image: Javier Carro

The Cathedral contains few works of art of high merit, but a preliminary walk round the Aisles, Transept, and Ambulatory behind the Choir will give a good idea of its general arrangement. Then return to view the paintings. The sacristan takes you round and unlocks the pictures. Do not let him hurry you.

Begin with the Left Aisle.

The Baptistery, on your left, contains a handsome font. right and left of the entry to it are admirable brasses. In the Baptistery itself on the left wall are two wings of a rather quaint triptych, representing St. Martin dividing his cloak with the beggar; St. Nicholas raising to life the three boys who had been salted for meat; St. Mary Magdalen with the pot of ointment (in the distance, as Penitent in the Desert); and St. Barbara with her tower; dated 1613. Also a rude Flemish picture (16th century) of the lives of St. Joachim and St. Anna, and their daughter the Blessed Virgin:—the main episodes are the Marriage of the Virgin, Birth of the Virgin, and Rejection of St. Joachim from the Temple, with other scenes in the background.

The end wall of the Baptistery has Peter Pourbus's masterpiece, a *triptych painted for the Guild of the Holy Sacrament, attached to the church of St. Sauveur, and allusive to their functions. The outer wings, when closed, represent the Miracle of the Mass of St. Gregory, when the Host, as he consecrated it, was changed into the bodily Presence of the Saviour, to silence a doubter. It thus shows in a visible form the tremendous mystery of Transubstantiation, in honour of which the Guild was founded. Behind, the Brothers of the Confraternity are represented (on the right wing) in attendance on the Pope, as spectators of the miracle.

One of them holds his triple crown. These may rank among the finest portraits by the elder Pourbus. They show the last stage in the evolution of native Flemish art before it was revolutionized by Rubens. The inner picture represents, in the centre, the Last Supper, or rather, the Institution of the Eucharist, to commemorate which fact the Guild was founded. The arrangement of the figures is in the old conventional order, round three sides of a table, with Judas in the foreground to the left. The wings contain Old Testament subjects of typical import, as foreshadowing the Eucharist. Left, Melchisedec giving bread and wine to Abraham; right, Elijah fed by the angel in the Wilderness. All the faces have still much of the old Flemish portrait character.

On the right wall are the wings of a picture, by F. Pourbus (the son), painted for the Guild of Shoemakers, whose chapel is adjacent. The inside contains portraits of the members. On the outside are their patrons, St. Crispinus and St. Crispianus, with their shoemakers' knives.

Also, an early Crucifixion, of the school of Cologne (about 1400), with St. Catherine holding her wheel and trampling on the tyrant Maximin, by whose orders she was executed, and St. Barbara with her tower. (These two also occur together in Memling's great triptych.) The picture is interesting as the only specimen in Bruges of the precursors of Van Eyck on the lower Rhine. The Baptistery contains, besides, a fine old candlestick, and a quaint ciborium (for the Holy Oil) with coloured reliefs of the Seven Joys of Mary (1536).

The vistas from the North Transept are impressive. It terminates in the Chapel of the Shoemakers' Guild, with a fine carved wooden door of about 1470, and good brasses, as well as an early crucifix. It is dedicated to the patron saints of the craft, and bears their arms, a boot.

The first two chapels in the Ambulatory (behind the Choir) have good screens.

The third Chapel encloses the tomb of Archbishop Carondelet, in alabaster, (1544,) a fine work of the Italian Renaissance. The Descent from the Cross by Claeissens, with the Crown of Thorns and the Holy Blood in the foreground: on the wings, St. Philip, and the donor, under the protection of (the canonized) Charlemagne. Near this is a *triptych by Dierick Bouts, (falsely ascribed to Memling) representing, in the centre, St. Hippolytus torn to pieces by four horses. (He was the jailor of St. Lawrence, who converted him: see Mrs. Jameson).

The faces show well the remarkable power of this bourgeois painter of Louvain. On the left wing are the donors; on the right wing Hippolytus confesses himself a Christian, and is condemned to martyrdom. Over the altar, retable, a Tree of Jesse, in carved woodwork, with the family of Our Lady: on the wings, (painted,) the legend of St. Hubert and the stag, and the legend of St. Lucy.

In the Apse is the Chapel of the Host.

The next chapel, of the Seven Sorrows, has a Mater Dolorosa of 1460 (copy of one at Rome); a fine *brass; and the *portrait of Philippe le Beau, known as Philippus Stok (father of Charles V), and bearing the collar of the Golden Fleece.

The Choir, (admirable architecturally,) contains the *stalls and arms of the Knights of the Golden Fleece, with good carved Misereres.

The Cathedral contains many other pictures of interest, which, however, do not fall within the scope of these Guides.

The Chambre des Marguilliers, or Churchwardens' Vestry, contains manuscripts and church furniture, sufficiently described by the sacristan.

In the Sacristy are still preserved the relics of St. Donatian, with accompanying notes as to their origin and significance.

We now continue onward to the Church of Our Lady, with the guide overleaf assuming you have just departed St. Salvator.

Church of Our Lady

[This church is open from 9:30am to 5:00pm, Monday to Saturday. On Sundays tours are taken from 1:30pm to 5pm.

While entry to the nave is free, the museum section – and hence most of the major artworks I note herein, makes a charge of 6 euros. Children under 12 however go free, while seniors and young people under 26 receive discounts.]

On leaving the Cathedral, go round the south side, which affords an excellent view of the chapels built out from the apse. Then take the little Rue du St. Esprit as far as the Church of Our Lady, which replaced a chapel, built by St. Boniface, the Apostle of Germany, in 744, and enclosed in the town in 909.

The Gothic facade and archways of the Church of Our Lady - Image: Bernt Rostad

Stand opposite it, in the small Place on the north side, to observe the somewhat shapeless architecture, the handsome brick tower crowned by a tall brick steeple, and the beautiful little *porch or "Paradise," built out from the main structure in flamboyant Gothic of the 15th century. The portal of this porch has been walled up, and the area is now used as a chapel, approached from the interior. Notice the delicate tracery of the windows, the fine finials and niches, and the charming gable-end.

The picturesque building with turrets to the left of the church was originally the mansion of the family Van der Gruuthuus, one of the principal medieval stocks of Bruges. It had a passage communicating with the family gallery in the church of Notre-Dame. The building, recently restored, is now in course of being fitted up for the Town Museum of Antiquities. A Museum of Lace is already installed in it; the entrance is by a doorway over the bridge to the left.

Church of our Lady Nave and Organ - Image: Paul Hermans

Enter the church, and walk straight into the Nave, below the great West Window, a spot which affords a good view of the centre of the church, the vaulted double Aisles, and the angular Apse. The Choir is shut off from the body of the church by a very ugly marble Rood-Screen (1722), still bearing its crucifix, and with a figure of Our Lady, patroness of the church, enshrined above its central arch. Rococo statues of the Twelve Apostles, with their well-known symbols (1618), are attached to the pillars. (Note these symbols: they recur in similar situations everywhere.) In spite of hideous disfigurements, the main portion of the interior is still a fine specimen of good middle Gothic architecture, mainly of the 14th century.

Walk up the outer left Aisle. The last bay is formed by the Baptistery, originally the porch, whose beautiful exterior we have already viewed. Its interior architecture is also very charming. It contains the Font, and the usual figure of the patron, St. John the Baptist. This Aisle terminates in an apsidal chapel (of the Holy Cross) containing inferior pictures of the 17th century, representing the history of a relic of the True Cross preserved here.

The inner left Aisle leads to the Ambulatory or passage at the back of the Choir. The Confessionals to the right have fairly good rococo carved woodwork, 1689. On the left is the handsome mediæval woodwork gallery (1474), belonging to the Van der Gruuthuus family, originally approached by a passage from their mansion behind. Beneath it, is a screen of delicate early Gothic architecture, with family escutcheons above the door.

The windows of the Apse have good modern stained glass.

On the left, at the entrance to the Apse, Pourbus's Adoration of the Shepherds, a winged picture, closed. The sacristan will open it. On the wings are, left, the donor, Sire Josse de Damhoudere, with his patron, St. Josse, and his four sons; right, his wife, Louise, with her five daughters, and her patron St. Louis of France, wearing his crown and robe of fleurs-de-lis, and holding the main de justice. He is represented older than is usual, or indeed historical, and in features somewhat resembles Henri IV. This is a fine picture for its master. On the outer wings are the cognate subjects, the Circumcision and the Adoration of the Magi, in grisaille.

The chapel in the Apse, formerly the Lady Chapel, now contains the Host. It has a gaudy modern altar for the monstrance.

In the South Ambulatory, over a doorway, Foundation of the Church of Santa Maria Maggiore at Rome, by Claeissens.

The chapel to the left contains the celebrated **tombs of Mary of Burgundy and Charles the Bold, her father. Mary was the wife of Maximilian, and died by a fall from her horse in 1482, when only twenty-five. Her **monument was designed and executed by Peter Beckere of Brussels, by order of her son Philippe le Beau, in 1502.

The sarcophagus is of black marble: the statue of the Princess, in gilt bronze, lies recumbent upon it. The style is intermediate between that of the later Middle Ages and of the full Renaissance. Beside it is the *tomb of Charles the Bold, of far less artistic value. Charles was buried at Nancy, after the fatal battle, but his body was transported to St. Donatian in this town by his descendant Charles V, and finally laid here beside his daughter by Philip II, who had this tomb constructed for his ancestor in imitation of that of Mary.

(I advise the visitor after seeing these tombs and the great chimney-piece of the Franc de Bruges to read up the history of Charles the Bold and his descendants, down to Charles V.)

The east wall of this chapel, beyond the tomb of Charles the Bold, has a fine picture of Our Lady of Sorrows, enthroned, surrounded by smaller subjects of the Seven Sorrows. Beginning at the left, the Circumcision, the Flight into Egypt, Christ lost by his parents in the Temple, the Way to Calvary, (with St. Veronica holding out her napkin,) the Crucifixion, (with Our Lady, St. John, and Mary Magdalen,) the Descent from the Cross, and the Deposition in the Tomb. A fine work of its sort, attributed to Mostart (or to Maubeuge).

On the west wall are two wings from a triptych by Pourbus, with tolerable portraits, (centre-piece destroyed,) and an early Flemish painting of the Deposition from the Cross (interesting for comparison with Roger van der Weyden and Gerard David). In the foreground lies the vessel containing the Holy Blood. On the wings are the Crucifixion and the Resurrection. The whole is very rudely painted. Outside are portraits of the donor and his wife and children, with their patrons St. James (staff and scallop) and St. Margaret (whose dragon just appears in the background).

Michelangelo's Madonna - Image: Artmechanic

On an arcade, a little further on, is a very early fresco (1350?) of a saint (St. Louis of France?), and also a dainty small relief (about 1500) of a donor, introduced by his patron, St. Peter, adoring Our Lady.

The end chapel of the right aisle, that of the Holy Sacrament, contains a celebrated and noble white marble **Madonna and

Child, by Michael Angelo, enshrined in a black marble niche. The pensive, grave, and graceful face, the exquisite modelling of the dainty naked Child, and the beautiful infantile pose of its left hand, all betray a design of Michelangelo, though the execution may possibly have been left to pupils.

But the modelling is softer and more feminine than is usual with this great sculptor, except in his early period. In this respect, it resembles most the unfinished Madonna in the Bargello at Florence. Condivi mentions that Peter Mouscron of Bruges ordered of Michael Angelo a Madonna and Child in bronze: he was probably mistaken as to the material: and we have here doubtless the work in question. Apart from its great artistic value, this exquisite group is interesting as affording another link between Flanders and Italy.

The same chapel also contains some good 17th century pictures.

Near the confessional, as we return towards the West End of the church, we find a good diptych of Herri met de Bles, of 1520, containing, left panel, an Annunciation, with all the conventional elements; to the left, as usual, is the angel Gabriel; to the right, Our Lady. These relative positions are never altered. The lilies in the pot, the desk and book, the bed with its furniture, the arcade in the background, and the rich brocade, are all constant features in pictures of this subject. Look out for them elsewhere.

The right panel has the Adoration of the Magi, with the Old, Middle-aged, and Young Kings, the last-named a Moor. This quaint and interesting work of a Flemish painter, with its archaic background, and its early Italian reminiscences, also betrays the influence of Dürer. Among the other pictures may be mentioned a triptych in an adjacent small chapel: the central panel shows the Transfiguration, with the three apostles below, Moses, Elias, and the Eternal Father above (perhaps by Jan Mostart). On the wings (much later, by P. Pourbus), are the portraits of the donor, his wife, and their patron saints.

Prominently displayed is a famous but overrated Crucifixion by Van Dyck. Though possessing beauty of conception and composition, the work has been spoiled somewhat by restorations.

The West Wall of the church has several large pictures of the later Renaissance, which can be sufficiently inspected on their merits by those who care for them. The best of them are the Adoration of the Magi by Seghers, and De Crayer's Adoration of the Infant Jesus. I do not propose to deal at length with later Flemish art till we reach Brussels and Antwerp: at Bruges, it is best to confine oneself to the introductory period of Flemish painting—that of the Burgundian princes. I will therefore only call attention here to the meaningless way in which huge pictures like B. van Orley's Crucifixion, with subsidiary scenes from the Passion, reproduce the form of earlier winged pictures, which becomes absurd on this gigantic scale.

The Church of Saint Jacob / Sint-Jakobsberk

[Open during daytime hours from around 9am to 5pm, with shorter hours for visiting tourists on Sunday to allow for the morning services]

This church stands in the street of the same name, conveniently near the Hôtel du Commerce. It is also referred to as the Church of Saint James. It is quite notable for housing the tombstone of the great artist Peter Paul Rubens.

It is a good old mediæval building (12th century, rebuilt 1457-1518), but hopelessly ruined by alterations in the 17th century, and now, as a fabric, externally and internally uninteresting. Its architecture is in the churchwarden style: its decoration in the upholsterer's.

The carved wooden pulpit is a miracle of bad taste (17th century), surpassed only by the part-coloured marble rood-screen. A few good pictures and decorative objects, however, occur among the mass of paintings ranged round its walls as in a gallery. The best is a panel of the old Flemish School (by Dierick Bouts, or more probably a pupil), in the left aisle, just beyond the second doorway.

It tells very naïvely the History of St. Lucy (see Mrs. Jameson). Left, she informs her mother that she is about to distribute her goods to the poor, who are visibly represented in a compact body asking alms behind her. Centre, she is hailed before the consul Paschasius by her betrothed, whom she refuses to marry.

She confesses herself a Christian, and is condemned to a life of shame. Right, she is dragged away to a house of ill-fame, the consul Paschasius accompanying; but two very stumpy oxen fail to move her. The Holy Ghost flits above her head. The details are good, but the figures very wooden and dated, 1480.

Beside it is an extravagant Lancelot Blondeel of St. Cosmo and St. Damian, the doctor saints, with surgical instruments and pots of ointment. The central picture shows their martyrdom.

Further on hangs a good Flemish triptych (according to Waagen, by Jan Mostart), representing, the prophecies of Christ's coming: centre, the Madonna and Child; with King Solomon below, from whom a genealogical tree rises to bear St. Joachim and St. Anna, parents of Our Lady. right and left of him, Balaam and Isaiah, who prophesied of the Virgin and Christ: with two Sibyls, universally believed in the Middle Ages to have also foretold the advent of the Saviour. The stem ends in the Virgin and Child. Left, the Tiburtine Sibyl showing the Emperor Augustus the vision of the glorious Virgin in the sky: right, St. John the Evangelist in Patmos beholding the Apocalyptic vision of the Woman clothed with the Sun. This is a fine work of its kind, and full of the prophetic ideas of the Middle Ages.

Pass round the Ambulatory and Choir to the first chapel at the east end of the right Aisle. It contains an altar with the Madonna and Child in Della Robbia ware, probably by Luca. Also, a fine tomb of Ferry de Gros and his two wives, the first of whom reposes by his side and the second beneath him. This is a good piece of early Renaissance workmanship (about 1530). The church also contains a few excellent later works by Pourbus and others, which need not be specified. This was the church of the Florentine merchants at Bruges (whence perhaps the Della Robbia) and particularly of the Portinari, who commissioned the great altar-piece by Van der Goes now in the Hospital of Santa Maria Nuova at Florence.

The other churches of Bruges need not detain the tourist, though all contain a few objects of interest for the visitor who has a week or two at his disposition.

Groeningemuseum

[The museum is closed on Mondays – between Tuesday and Sunday the opening hours are from 9:30am to 5pm.

Adults pay an admission fee of 8 euros, with children under 12 years admitted free. Those of senior age or under 26 receive a discounted rate of 6 euros.]

The Groeningemuseum is situated at Djiver, and was conceived as a means of uniting the hitherto scattered artworks of Bruges into a single, encompassing destination. Among the institutions it replaced almost a century ago was the renowned Academy of the Rue St. Catherine.

While the museum encompasses many neoclassical works, as well as modern art from the recent post-World War 2 era, the artistic centerpieces without doubt belong to Jan van Eyck, Hans Memling and the other Flemish Primitive era painters. I have chosen to describe in detail the most notable works showcased in the rooms of this altogether reasonable gallery.

Jan van Eyck. **Altar-piece, ordered by George van der Palen, for the High Altar of the original Cathedral of St. Donatian, of which he was a canon. The centre of the picture is occupied by the Madonna and Child, the face of Our Lady somewhat recalling German models. She sits in the apse of a church, probably St. Donatian. The Child, whom it is the fashion to describe as "aged-looking," fondles a parrot and grasps a bunch of flowers. To the left stands St. Donatian the Archbishop, patron saint of the church for which this altar-piece was painted. He bears his usual symbol, the wheel with five lighted candles (as in the beautiful panel by Gerard David in the National Gallery at London). This is a fine and finely-painted figure. To the right, St. George, in full armour, admirably represented, but in an affected attitude, lifts his casque somewhat jauntily as he presents his namesake the Canon George to Our Lady. In all this we get a touch of Burgundian courtliness: the event is represented as a state ceremonial. With his left hand the Saint supports his Red Cross banner. The portrait of the kneeling Canon himself,—asthmatic, pudding-faced—is very admirable and life-like, but by no means flattered. He grips his prayer-book with an old man's tremulous hand. (For a profound criticism of this fine picture, see Conway.) The insipid Madonna, the rather foolish St. George, the fine portrait of the Canon, are all typical of Van Eyck's manner. The accessories of architecture, decoration, and background, should also be carefully noted. The capitals of the columns and the knobs of glass in the window, as well as St. George's costume, are elaborated in Van Eyck's finest fashion.

(2.) Jan van Eyck. *Portrait of his wife, painted for presentation to the Bruges Guild of Painters, together with one of the artist himself, now undiscoverable. This is a fine though evidently unflattered portrait of a capable housewife, very stiffly arrayed in her best church-going costume. It deserves close inspection.

Above it, (3.) Head of Christ, ascribed to Jan van Eyck, but in reality a poor and reduced copy of the picture at Berlin.

(4.) Memling. **Triptych painted for Willem Moreel or Morelli, a member of a wealthy Savoyard family settled at Bruges. Like Jan van Eyck's portrait of the two Arnolfini in London, and Hugo van der Goes's triptych of the Portinari at Florence, this picture marks well the cosmopolitan character of old Bruges. In the central panel, St. Christopher (whose altar in the church of St. Jacques it adorned) wades with his staff through the water, feeling as he goes the increasing burden of the Christ-Child on his shoulder. (For the legend, see Mrs. Jameson.) To the left, above, is the diminutive figure of the hermit with his lantern, which always accompanies St. Christopher. The left foreground of the picture is occupied by St. Maurus, in his Benedictine costume; to the right is St. Giles (St. Egidius) the hermit, with the wounded doe, the arrow piercing the arm of the saint.

The left wing represents the donor, Willem Moreel, under the care of his patron, St. William, who wears a hermit's dress above his coat of armour. (When a saint places his hand on a votary's shoulder it usually implies that the votary is a namesake.) Behind are Moreel's five sons. All these portraits, but particularly that of the donor and his eldest son, who closely resembles him, are admirable. The right wing represents the donor's wife, Barbara, under the protection of her patron, St. Barbara, with her tower, showing as usual three windows (emblematic of the Holy Trinity). Behind the lady are her two daughters, one of whom is habited as a Benedictine nun, whence, doubtless, the introduction of St. Maurus into the main altar-piece. This fine triptych originally decorated an altar of St. Christopher in Moreel's private chapel in the church of St. Jacques.

One of his daughters is the "Sibylla Sambetha" represented at the Hospital. The wings at the back represent in grisaille St. John the Baptist with the lamb, and St. George with the dragon. It was usual to paint the outer wings in grisaille or in low tones of colour, so that the splendour of the interior hues might burst upon the spectator as the triptych was opened.

Gerard David has a *triptych, painted for Jean des Trompes, for the High Altar of the lower chapel of the Holy Blood. The central panel represents the Baptism of Christ. In the middle, the Saviour wades in the water of a diminutive Jordan, where the concentric circles show the increased careful study of nature.

On the right-hand side of the picture, St. John-Baptist, patron saint of the donor, pours water on his head. The relative positions of these two figures, and of the angel to the left holding a robe, are conventional: they have descended from a very early period of art. (In the Ravenna mosaics, the place of the angel is filled by the river-god of the Jordan with his urn, afterwards transformed and Christianized into an angel with a towel. Look out in future for similar arrangements.) The central figures are weak; but the robe of the angel is painted with Flemish minuteness. So are the flowers and leaves of the foreground. Above, the dove descends upon the head of the Saviour, while the Eternal Father pronounces from the skies the words, "Behold my Beloved Son in whom I am well pleased."

In the background are two other episodes: on the left is the preaching of St. John-Baptist (where Oriental costumes indicate the heathen); right, St. John-Baptist pointing out Christ to his disciples with the words, "Behold the Lamb of God." The distance shows two towns and a fine landscape. Observe the admirable painting of the trees, with their good shadows; also the ivy climbing up the trunk of one to the right. This picture is among the earliest in which the gloom of a wood is accurately represented: in many other respects it well illustrates the rise of landscape-painting. (For an exhaustive criticism, see Conway.) The left wing has a portrait of the donor, with his other patron, St. John the Evangelist, holding the cup. Beside the donor kneels his little son Philip. This portrait, the face and foot of the Evangelist, the fur of the donor's robe, the crane in the background, and many other accessories deserve close attention.

Two figures in the background dimly foreshadow Teniers. The right wing has a portrait of the donor's wife, Elizabeth, with her four daughters. Behind her stands her patroness, St. Elizabeth of Hungary, in Franciscan robes, with the crown on her head and the double crown and book in her hands, as on the statuette at the door of the Béguinage. The painting of a rosary here is excellent. The outer wings (turn them back) show, on the left, the Madonna and Child with a bunch of grapes; on the right, the donor's second wife Madeleine, introduced by her patroness, St. Mary Madeleine, who holds the alabaster pot of ointment. By the lady's side kneels her daughter. The background consists of a view, probably in the Bruges of that period. Painted about 1507.

Arguably the most striking work by Gerard David, The Punishment of the Unjust Judge, is present. These two panels are of a type commonly set up in courts of justice as a warning to evil-doers. They were ordered by the Bruges magistracy. You will see a similar pair by Dierick Bouts in Brussels. The story, a horrid one, is taken from Herodotus. Sisamnes was a judge in Persia whom King Cambyses detected receiving a bribe and ordered to be flayed alive. The king then stretched his skin on the seat of judgment, and appointed the son of Sisamnes to sit in his father's place, that he might remember to avoid a like fate. The first picture represents, in the background, the bribery. In the foreground, King Cambyses, in a rich embroidered robe, demonstrates on his fingers the guilt of the unjust judge. Sisamnes is seized on his tribunal by a man of the people; courtiers, lawyers, and burgesses looking on. The expression on his face and the painting of all the accessories is admirable.

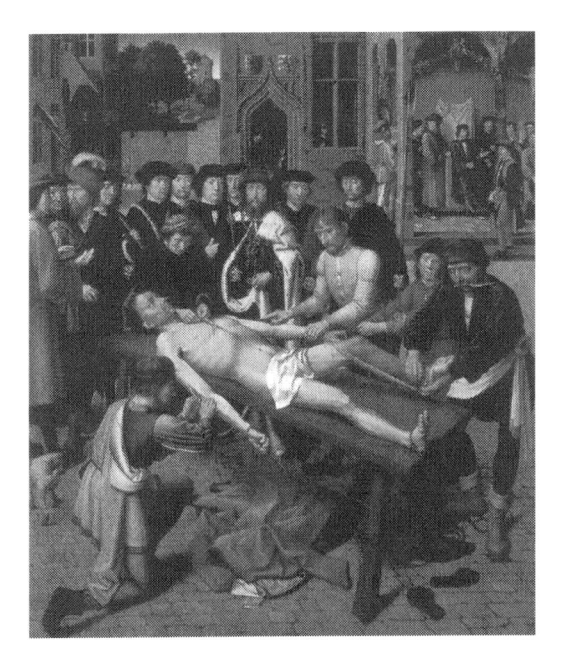

In the second picture we have the flaying of the unjust judge, a horrible scene, powerfully rendered. Cambyses stands by, holding his sceptre, surrounded by courtiers who recall the last age of the Burgundian dominion. In the background (as a subsequent episode) the son of Sisamnes is seen sitting in his father's place: behind him hangs the skin of the father. Architecture, landscape, ropes, and all other accessories of this painful picture should be carefully noted.

15. J. Prévost. Last Judgment. Below, the dead are rising, half naked, from the tomb, girt only with their shrouds; the good receiving garments from angels, and the bad hurried away to a very Flemish and unimpressive Hell. Above, Christ as Judge holds the sword. Two angels blow out the words of blessing or malediction. On the spectator's left, Our Lady shows the breast that suckled the Redeemer. Behind her are St. Peter with the key, St. Paul with the sword, St. Bartholomew with the knife, and other saints. On the right are St. John-Baptist with the lamb, King David with the harp, Moses, horned (as always), with the tables of the law, and a confused group of saints. This picture is rather curious than beautiful. Above it is a later treatment of the same subject by Van Coornhuuse, interesting for

comparison as showing the usual persistence of types and the conventional grouping of the individual figures. Compare especially the corresponding personages in the lower left-hand corners.

A few other pictures deserve passing notice. There is Death and the Miser, of the School of Quentin Matsys. Lancelot Blondeel, the architect of the great chimney-piece of the Franc de Bruges, represents St. Luke painting Our Lady, in one of the fantastic frames in which this painter delighted. Blondeel also has a St. George and the Dragon, with the Princess Cleodolind looking on. Around it are four smaller scenes of his martyrdom: (he was boiled, burnt with torches, dragged by a horse, and finally decapitated).

Other works include a good diptych of the Flemish school, by an unknown contemporary of Gerard David. It represents, left, a donor, with his patron St. John the Almoner, holding his symbol, a sheaf of corn. On the right, his wife with her patroness, St. Godeliva. 28, is an Adoration of the Magi, where the Three Kings again illustrate the three ages of man and the three continents. Beside it is a Nativity which exhibits all the traditional features already noted.

You may also behold a tolerably good Adoration of the Magi, of the German School, 15th century. Note once more the Three Kings, of whom the youngest is a Moor. Further drawings by Jan van Eyck of St. Barbara should be closely inspected. She holds a palm of martyrdom. In the background, workmen build her tower. It is interesting as a scene of real life at this period. This is a replica of the well-known picture at Antwerp. To the right, two coloured drawings by Gerard David from the life of St. John-Baptist. Above these hangs a tolerable P. Pourbus of the Last

Judgment, valuable for comparison with the two previous treatments of the same subject on the principal wall. Go from one to the other once or twice. Later painters of the Renaissance use this solemn theme as a mere excuse for obtruding the nude—and often the vulgar nude—into churches. On the same wall are a good triptych in grisaille by P. Pourbus (Way to Calvary, Descent from the Cross, Resurrection: from Notre-Dame at Damme), and other pictures.

The remaining walls have portraits and other works, from the 17th century downwards, most of which need no explanation. A few of them, indeed, are not without merit. But, as I have before observed, it is best in medieval Bruges to confine oneself to the 13th, 14th, 15th, and early 16th centuries, leaving the rise of the Renaissance, and the later Flemish School of painting, to occupy us at Antwerp, where they can be studied to far greater advantage.

As mentioned earlier, both within and outside the Groeningemuseum there are many artworks of later periods. Cubist and expressionist influences abound, with notable Magritte and Delvaux pieces providing interesting if comparatively trivial differentiation to the Medieval and Renaissance era works which outstrip them in significance.

Historical Notes on Belgium

Within this and other guidebooks in the series, the separate Introductions to the various towns deal rather with their origins than offer a blow by blow historical account. I have laid stress chiefly on the industrial and municipal facts, which in Belgium are all-important. I add here, however, a few general notes on the political history of the country as a whole, with a chiefly dynastic bent. These may serve for reference, or at least as reminders; and in particular they should be useful as giving some information about the originals of portraits in the various galleries.

The two portions of the modern kingdom of Belgium with which we are most concerned in this Guide are the County of Flanders and the Duchy of Brabant. The first was originally a fief of France; the second, a component member of the Empire. They were commercially wealthier than the other portions of the Gallo-German borderland which is now Belgium; they were also the parts most affected by the Burgundian princes; on both which accounts, they are still by far the richest in works of art, alike in architecture, in painting, and in sculpture.

The vast Frankish dominions of the Merovingians and of the descendants of Charlemagne—of the Merwings and Karlings, to be more strictly Teutonic—showed at all times a tendency to break up into two distinct realms, known as the Eastern and Western Kingdoms (Austria—not, of course, in the modern sense—and Neustria). These kingdoms were not artificial, but based on a real difference of race and speech. The Eastern Kingdom (Franken or Franconia) where the Frankish and Teutonic blood was purest, became first the Empire, in the restricted sense, and later Germany and Austria (in part). The Western Kingdom (Neustria) where Celtic or Gallic blood predominated, and where the speech was Latin, or (later) French, became in time the Kingdom of France. But between these two Francias, and especially during the period of unrest, there existed a certain number of middle provinces, sometimes even a middle kingdom, known from its first possessor, Lothar, son of Charlemagne, as Lotharingia or Lorraine. Of these middle provinces, the chief northern members were Flanders, Brabant, Hainault, and Liège.

Flanders in the early Middle Ages was a fief of France; it included not only the modern Belgian provinces of East and West Flanders, but also French Flanders, that is to say the

Department of the Nord and part of the Pas de Calais. As early as the Treaty of Verdun (843), the land of Flanders was assigned to Neustria. But the county, as we know it, really grew up from the possessions of a noble family at Bruges and Sluys, the head of which was originally known as Forester or Ranger. In 862, the King of France, as suzerain, changed this title to that of Count, in the person of Baldwin Bras-de-Fer (Baldwin I.). Baldwin was also invested with the charge of the neighbouring coast of France proper, on tenure of defending it against the Norman pirates.

In 1006, his descendant, Baldwin IV., seized the Emperor's town of Valenciennes; and having shown his ability to keep his booty, he was invested by the Franconian Henry II. with this district as a fief, so that he thus became a feudatory both of France and of the Empire. He was also presented with Ghent and the Isles of Zealand. Baldwin V. (1036) added to the growing principality the districts of Alost, Tournai, and Hainault. The petty dynastic quarrels of the 11th century are far too intricate for record here; in the end, the domains of the Counts were approximately restricted to what we now know as Flanders proper. A bare list of names and dates must suffice for this epoch:—Baldwin V. (1036-1067); Baldwin VI. (1067-1070); Robert II. (1093-1111); and Baldwin VII. (1111-1119).

After this date, the native line having become extinct, the county was held by foreign elective princes, under whom the power of the towns increased greatly. Among these alien Counts, the most distinguished was Theodoric (in French, Thierry; in German, Dietrich; or in Dutch, Dierick) of Alsace, who was a distinguished Crusader, and the founder of the Chapel of the Holy Blood at Bruges (which see).

Under Baldwin of Hainault (1191-1194) Artois was ceded to France, together with St. Omer and Hesdin. Henceforth, Ghent superseded Arras as the capital. Baldwin IX. (1194-1206) became a mighty Crusader, and founded the Latin Empire of Constantinople. Indeed, the Crusades were largely manned and managed by Flemings. He was followed in Flanders by his two daughters, Johanna and Margaret, under whose rule the cities gained still greater privileges. Margaret's son, Guy de Dampierre, was the creature of Philippe IV. of France, who endeavoured to rule Flanders through his minister, Châtillon. The Flemings answered by just revolt, and fought the famous Battle of the Spurs near Courtrai, already described, against the French interlopers (see Bruges). In 1322, Louis de Nevers (Louis I.) became Count, and provoked by his Gallicising and despotic tendencies the formidable rebellion under Van Artevelde (see Ghent). The quarrel between the league of burghers and their lord continued more or less during the reigns of Count Louis II. (1346) and Louis III., who died in 1385, leaving one daughter, Margaret, married to Philip the Bold (Philippe-le-Hardi) of Burgundy.

The political revolution caused in Flanders and Brabant by the accession of the Burgundian dynasty was so deep-reaching that a few words must be devoted to the origin and rise of this powerful family, a branch of the royal Valois of France. The old Kingdom of Burgundy had of course been long extinct; but its name was inherited by two distinct principalities, the Duchy of Burgundy, which formed part of France, and the County of Burgundy (Franche Comté), which was a fief of the Empire. In the 14th century, a new middle kingdom, like the earlier Lotharingia, seemed likely to arise by the sudden growth of a practically independent power in this debatable land between France and Germany.

Anonymous portrait of John le Bon

In 1361, the Duchy of Burgundy fell in to the crown of France; and in order, as he thought, to secure its union with the central authority, John the Good of France (Jean-le-Bon), during the troublous times after the Treaty of Bretigny, conferred it as a fief upon his son, Philippe de Valois (Philip the Bold, or Philippe-le-Hardi) who married Margaret of Flanders, thus uniting two of the greatest vassal principalities of the French crown. In 1385, on the death of Louis III., Philip succeeded to the County of Flanders, now practically almost an independent state. After him reigned three other princes of his family.

John the Fearless (Jean-sans-Peur, 1404-1419) will be remembered by visitors to Paris as the builder of the Porte Rouge at Notre-Dame de Paris. Philip the Good (Philippe-le-Bon, 1419-1467) was the patron of Van Eyck and Memling. (His portrait by Roger van der Weyden is in the Antwerp Gallery.) Charles the Bold (Charles-le-Téméraire, 1467-1477) raised the power of the house to its utmost pitch, and then destroyed it. (His portrait by Memling is in the Brussels Gallery.) Contrary, however, to the belief of John the Good, the princes of the Valois dynasty in Burgundy, instead of remaining loyal to the crown of France, became some of its most dangerous and dreaded rivals.

All these Dukes, as French princes, played at the same time an important part in the affairs of France. They also won, by marriage, by purchase, by treaty, or by conquest, large territories within the Empire, including most of modern Belgium and Holland, together with much that is now part of France. They were thus, like their Flemish predecessors, vassals at once of the Emperor and the French king; but they were really more powerful than either of their nominal over-lords; for their central position between the two jealous neighbours gave them great advantages, while their possession of the wealthy cities of the Low Countries made them into the richest princes in mediæval Europe. It was at their opulent and ostentatious court that Van Eyck and Memling painted the gorgeous pictures which still preserve for us some vague memory of this old-world splendour. At the same time, the increased power of the princes, who could draw upon their other dominions to suppress risings in Flanders, told unfavourably upon the liberties of the cities. The Burgundian dominion thus sowed the seeds of the Spanish despotism.

Jean-sans-Peur was murdered by the Dauphin, afterwards Charles VII.; and this cousinly crime threw his son, Philippe-le-Bon, into the arms of the English. It was the policy of Burgundy and Flanders, indeed, to weaken the royal power by all possible means. Philip supported the English cause in France for many years; and it was his defection, after the Treaty of Arras in 1435, that destroyed the chances of Henry VI. on the Continent. The reign of Philippe-le-Bon, we saw, was the Augustan age of the Burgundian dynasty. (Fully to understand Burgundian art, however, you must visit Dijon as well as Brabant and Flanders.) Under Charles the Bold, the most ambitious prince of the Burgundian house, the power of the Dukes was raised for a time to its highest pitch, and then began to collapse suddenly. A constant rivalry existed between Charles and his nominal suzerain, Louis XI. It was Charles's dream to restore or re-create the old Burgundian kingdom by annexing Lorraine, with its capital, Nancy, and conquering the rising Swiss Confederacy.

He would thus have consolidated his dominions in the Netherlands with his discontinuous Duchy and County of Burgundy. He had even designs upon Provence, then as yet an independent county. Louis XI. met these attempts to create a rival state by a policy of stirring up enemies against his too powerful feudatory. In his war with the Swiss, Charles was signally defeated in the decisive battles at Granson and Morat, in 1476. In the succeeding year, he was routed and killed at Nancy, whither the Swiss had gone to help René, Duke of Lorraine, in his effort to win back his Duchy from Charles. The conquered Duke was buried at Nancy, but his body was afterwards brought to Bruges by his descendant, the Emperor Charles V., and now reposes in the splendid tomb which we have seen at Notre-Dame in that city.

This war had important results. It largely broke down the power of Burgundy. Charles's daughter, Mary, kept the Low Countries and the County of Burgundy (Imperial); but the Duchy (French) reverted to the crown of France, with which it was ever after associated. The scheme of a great Middle Kingdom thus came to an end; and the destinies of the Low Countries were entirely altered.

We have next to consider the dynastic events by which the Low Countries passed under the rule of the House of Hapsburg. In 1477, Mary of Burgundy succeeded her father Charles as Countess of Flanders, Duchess of Brabant, etc. In the same year she was married to Maximilian of Austria, King of the Romans, son of the Emperor Frederic III. (or IV.). Maximilian was afterwards elected Emperor on his father's death. The children of this marriage were Philip the Handsome (Philippe-le-Beau, or le-Bel; Philippus Stok), who died in 1506, and Margaret of Austria. Philip, again, married Johanna (Juana) the Mad, of Castile, and thus became King of Castile, in right of his wife. The various steps by which these different sovereignties were cumulated in the person of Philip's son, Charles V., are so important to a proper comprehension of the subject that I advise you seek out a family tree illustration in other to fully comprehend their significance and centrality.

During the lifetime of Maximilian, who was afterwards Emperor, Mary, and her son Philippe-le-Beau, ruled at first in the Low Countries (for the quarrel between Maximilian and Bruges over the tutorship of Philippe, see p. 27). After the death of Isabella of Castile, Ferdinand retired to Aragon, and Philippe ruled Castile on behalf of his insane wife, Juana. Philippe died in 1506, and his sister, Margaret of Austria, then ruled as Regent in the Netherlands (for Charles) till her death in 1530. Charles V., born at Ghent in 1500, was elected to the Empire after his grandfather, Maximilian I., and thus became at once Emperor, King of Spain, Duke of Austria, and ruler of the Low Countries.

(In 1516 he succeeded Ferdinand in the Kingdom of Spain, and in 1519 was elected Emperor.)

The same series of events carried the Netherlands, quite accidentally, under Spanish rule. For Charles was an absolutist, who governed on essentially despotic principles. His conduct towards Ghent in 1539 brought affairs to a crisis. The Emperor, in pursuance of his plans against France, had demanded an enormous subsidy from the city, which the burgesses constitutionally refused to grant, meeting the unjust extortion by open rebellion. They even entered into negotiations with François Ier; who, however, with the base instinct of a brother absolutist, betrayed their secret to his enemy the Emperor. Charles actually obtained leave from François to march a Spanish army through France to punish the Flemings, and arrived with a powerful force before the rebellious city. The Ghenters demanded pardon; but Charles, deeply incensed, entered the town under arms, and took up his abode there in triumph.

Alva, his ruthless Spanish commander (portrait in the Brussels Gallery), suggested that the town should be utterly destroyed; but the Emperor could not afford to part with his richest and most populous city, nor could even he endure to destroy his birth-place. He contented himself with a terrible vengeance, beheading the ringleaders, banishing the minor patriots, and forfeiting the goods of all suspected persons. The city was declared guilty of lèse-majesté, and the town magistrates, with the chiefs of the Guilds, were compelled to appear before Charles with halters round their necks, and to beg for pardon. The Emperor also ordered that no magistrate of Ghent should ever thenceforth appear in public without a halter, a badge which became with time a mere silken decoration. The privileges of the city were at the same time abolished, and the famous old bell, Roland, was removed from the Belfry.

Thenceforth Charles treated the Netherlands as a conquered Spanish territory. He dissolved the monastery of St. Bavon, and erected on its site the great Citadel, which he garrisoned with Spaniards, to repress the native love of liberty of the Flemings (see Ghent). In subsequent risings of the Low Countries, the Spaniards' Castle, the stronghold of the alien force, was the first point to be attacked; and on it depended the issue of freedom or slavery in the Netherlands. Charles also established the Inquisition, which is said to have put to death no fewer than 100,000 persons.

In 1555, the Emperor abdicated in favour of his son Philip, known as Philip II. of Spain. But his brother Ferdinand, to whom he had resigned his Austrian dominions, was elected Emperor (having been already King of the Romans) as Ferdinand I. From his time forth, the Empire became more exclusively German, so that its connexion with Rome was almost forgotten save as a historic myth, degenerating into the mere legal fiction of a Holy Roman Empire, with nothing Roman in it. Thus, the Netherlands alone of the earlier Burgundian heritage remained in the holding of the Austrian kings of Spain, who ruled them nominally as native sovereigns, but practically as Spaniards and aliens by means of imported military garrisons.

Philip II.—austere, narrow, domineering, fanatical—remained only four years in the Netherlands, and then retired to Spain, appointing his half-sister, Margaret of Parma (illegitimate daughter of Charles V.), regent of the Low Countries (1559-1567). She resided in the Ancienne Cour at Brussels. Her minister, Granvella, Bishop of Arras, made himself so unpopular, and the measures taken against the Protestants were so severe, that the cities, ever the strongholds of liberty, showed signs of revolution. They objected to the illegal maintenance of a Spanish standing army, and also to the Inquisition. In April, 1567, as a consequence of the discontents, the Duke of Alva was sent with 10,000 men as lieutenant-general to the Netherlands, to suppress what was known as the Beggars' League (Les Gueux), now practically headed by the Prince of Orange (William the Silent). Alva entered Brussels with his Spanish and Italian mercenaries and treacherously seized his two suspected antagonists, Count Egmont and Count Hoorn.

The patriotic noblemen were imprisoned at Ghent, in the Spaniards' Castle, were condemned to death, and finally beheaded in the Grand' Place at Brussels. (For fuller details of the great revolutionary movement thus inaugurated, see Motley's Rise of the Dutch Republic, and Juste's Le Comté d'Egmont et le Comté de Hornes.) Alva also established in Brussels his infamous "Council of Troubles," which put to death in cold blood no less than 20,000 inoffensive burghers. His cold and impassive cruelty led to the Revolt of the United Provinces in 1568—a general movement of all the Spanish Netherlands (as they now began to be called) to throw off the hateful yoke of Spain. Under the able leadership of William of Orange, the Flemings besieged and reduced the Spaniards' Castle at Ghent. In the deadly struggle for freedom which ensued, the Northern Provinces (Holland), aided by their great natural advantages for defence among the flooded marshes of the Rhine delta, succeeded in casting off their allegiance to Philip. They were then known as the United Netherlands. The long and heroic contest of the Southern Provinces (Belgium) against the Spanish oppressor was not equally successful.

A desperate struggle for liberty met with little result, and the Spanish sovereigns continued to govern their Belgian dominions like a conquered country. In 1578, Alessandro Farnese, Duke of Parma (son of Margaret), was sent as Governor to the Netherlands, where he remained in power till 1596. In the prosecution of the war against the Northern Provinces (Holland) he besieged Antwerp, and took it after fourteen months in 1585. In the "Spanish Fury" which followed, Antwerp was almost destroyed, and all its noblest buildings ruined. Nevertheless, under Parma's rule, the other cities recovered to a certain extent their municipal freedom; though the country as a whole was still treated as a vanquished province.

The next great landmark of Belgian history is the passage of the Spanish Netherlands under Austrian rule. The first indefinite steps towards this revolution were taken in 1598, when Philip II. ceded the country as a fief to his daughter the Infanta Isabella

(Clara Isabella Eugenia) on her marriage with Albert, Archduke of Austria, who held the provinces as the Spanish Governor. (Portraits of Albert and Isabella by Rubens in the Brussels Gallery.) The new rulers made the country feel to a certain extent that it was no longer treated as a mere disobedient Spanish appanage. After the troubles of the Revolt, and the cruel destruction of Antwerp by Parma, trade and manufactures began to revive.

Albert and Isabella were strongly Catholic in sentiment; and it was under their régime that the greater part of the rococo churches of Antwerp and other cities were built, in the showy but debased taste of the period, and decorated with large and brilliantly-coloured altar-pieces. They also induced Rubens to settle in the Netherlands, appointed him Court painter, and allowed him to live at Antwerp, where the trade of the Low Countries was still largely concentrated. During their vice-royalty, however, Brussels became more than ever the recognised capital of the country, and the seat of the aristocracy.

After Albert's death in 1621, the Netherlands reverted to Spain, and a dull period, without either art or real local history, supervened, though the wars of the 17th and 18th centuries were in great part fought out over these unfortunate provinces, "the cockpit of Europe."

The campaigns of Marlborough and Prince Eugene are too well-known as part of English and European history to need recapitulation here. At the end of the War of the Spanish Succession, the Peace of Rastadt, in 1714, assigned the Spanish Netherlands to Austria, thus entailing upon the unhappy country another hundred years of foreign domination.

Nevertheless, the Austrian Netherlands, as they were thenceforth called (in contradistinction to the "United Netherlands" or Holland), were on the whole tolerably well governed by the Austrian Stadtholders, who held their court at Brussels, and who were usually relations of the Imperial family. Few memorials, however, of Maria Theresa, of Joseph II., or of Léopold II. now exist in Belgium, and those few are not remarkable for beauty. It was during this relatively peaceful and law-abiding time, on the other hand, that the Upper Town of Brussels was laid out in its existing form by Guimard. As a whole, the Belgian provinces were probably better governed under Austrian rule than under any other régime up to the period of the existing independent and national monarchy.

The French Revolutionists invaded Belgium in 1794, and committed great havoc among historical buildings at Bruges and elsewhere. Indeed, they did more harm to the arts of the Netherlands than anybody else, except the Spaniards and the modern "restorers." They also divided Belgium into nine departments; and Napoleon half sneeringly, half cynically, justified the annexation on the ground that the Low Countries were the alluvial deposit of French rivers. The Belgian States formed part of Napoleon's composite empire till 1814, when these Southern Provinces were assigned by the Treaty of London to Holland. In 1815, during the Hundred Days, the Allied Armies had their headquarters at Brussels, and the decisive battle against Napoleon was fought at Waterloo. The Congress of Vienna once more affirmed the union of Belgium with Holland; they remained as one kingdom till the first revolutionary period in 1830.

The Southern Provinces then successfully seceded from the Dutch monarchy: indeed, the attempted fusion of semi-French and Catholic Belgium with purely Teutonic and Protestant Holland was one of those foredoomed failures so dear to diplomacy. A National Congress elected Léopold of Saxe-Coburg as King of the Belgians (Roi des Belges), and the crown is now held by his son, Léopold II. For nearly seventy years Belgium has thus enjoyed, for the first time in its history, an independent and relatively popular government of its own choosing. The development of its iron and coal industries during this epoch has vastly increased its wealth and importance; while the rise of Antwerp as a great European port has also done much to develop its resources. At the present day Belgium ranks as one of the most thickly populated, richest, and on the whole most liberal-minded countries of Europe. Its neutrality is assured by the Treaty of London, and its army exists only to repel invasion in case that neutrality should ever be violated.

Much of the country suffered greatly during the two World Wars of the 20th century. The First World War, which saw Belgium as a bulwark against the military offenses of the German Empire, saw great damage and bombardment upon the civic centres, with Antwerp particularly badly damaged in the conflict. Many towns, such as Ypres, would become inextricably associated with the carnage and conflict.

The famed retrieval of the Ghent altarpiece and its panels

The Second World War was, fortuitously, less damaging upon the many artistic and architectural attainments around the country. The occupied cities avoided catastrophic damage, the hardship mainly wrought by the citizenry rather than the established, physically manifest culture. Matters were both helped and hindered by the attention to art by the fascist invaders: while more fastidious with art than a typical aggressor, the Nazis would also set about hiding them. Over the course of years after the war, a large proportion of artworks were successfully restored or retrieved. Most notably of all was the retrieval of the Ghent Alterpiece from a salt mine in Altausee after the hostilities ended. Having been placed there by Axis forces under orders from Hitler, the recovered panels were displayed to great media attention at the time. The entire escapade was given a recent treatment in Hollywood, in the motion picture *The Monuments Men*.

Given the immensity and scale of the death, many soldiers and war dead were buried in Flanders. The area of Flanders Fields were particularly associated with the First World War, with the poppies growing there becoming synonymous with the bloodshed. An American cemetery bearing the name Flanders Field is where a total of 368 soldiers were buried, and has become a noted visitor destination for those interested in modern wartime history.

Across Belgian cities, comparatively faithful renovation projects ensued after the conclusion of World War 2. Accessibility to the major civic and cultural centres of Belgium became easier with the aid of modern advances in transportation, while dedicated art historians within and outside the city universities successfully brought the myriad artworks to justifiably good housing. Successive renovations, improved means of storage, and better education on the fragility of the works described – together with a general absence of conflict – mean the past seventy and more years have seen the twin Flemish treasures of art and architecture treated with relative fastidiousness. It is hoped that this happy state of affairs persists well into the 21st century and beyond, to the benefit and promulgation of fine art and culture.

Printed in Great Britain
by Amazon